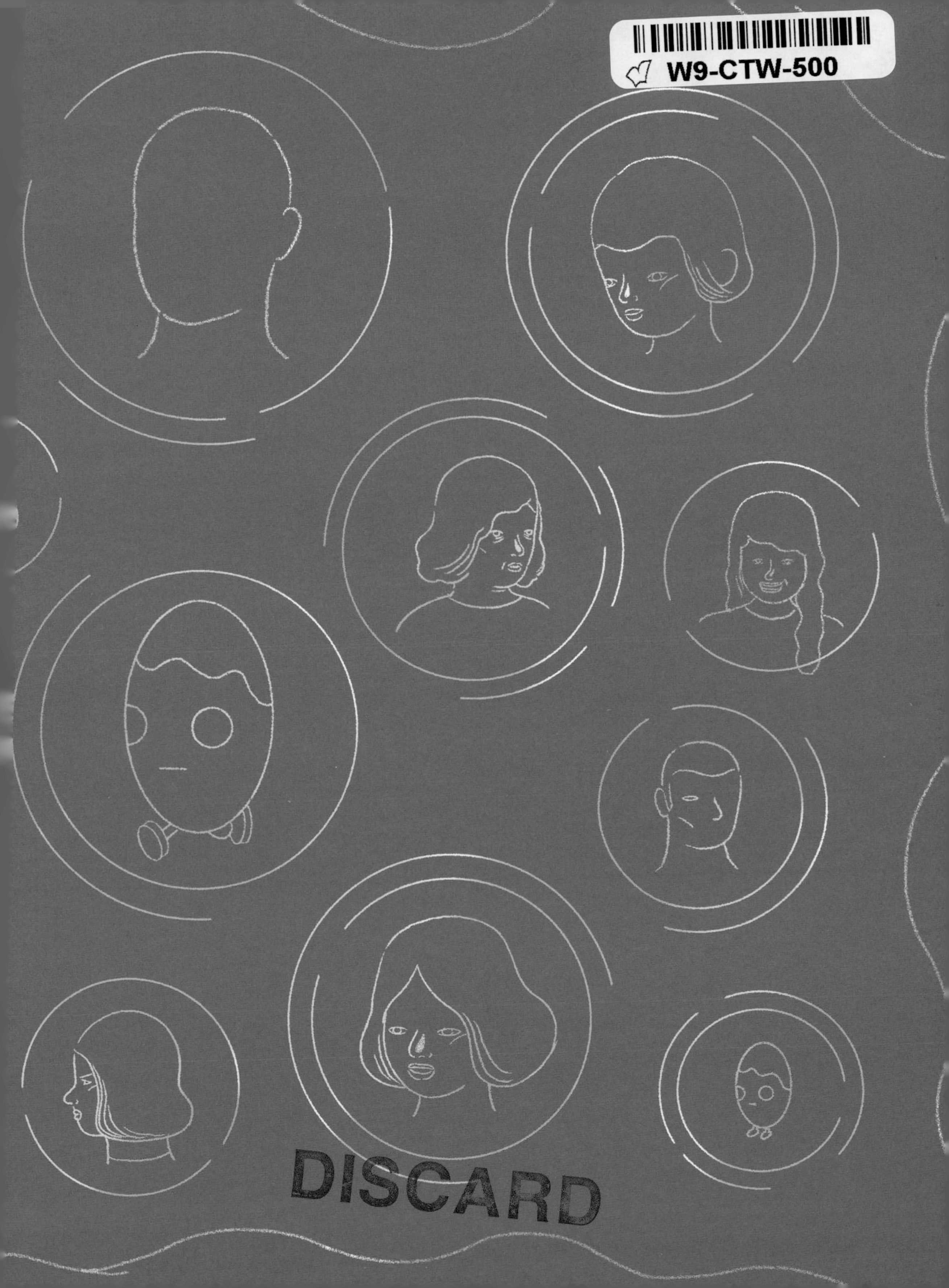

AFTER A McBUR

FANTAGRAPHICS

NOON
T
GER'S

ANA GALVAŇ

Fantagraphics Books Inc.
7563 Lake City Way NE
Seattle, Washington, 98115
www.fantagraphics.com

Translated from Spanish by Jamie Richards
Editor / Associate Publisher: Eric Reynolds
Book Design: Ana Galváñ with Keeli McCarthy
Production: Paul Baresh
Publisher: Gary Groth

ISBN 978-1-68396-484-1
Library of Congress
Control Number: 2021937422

First printing: November 2021
Printed in China

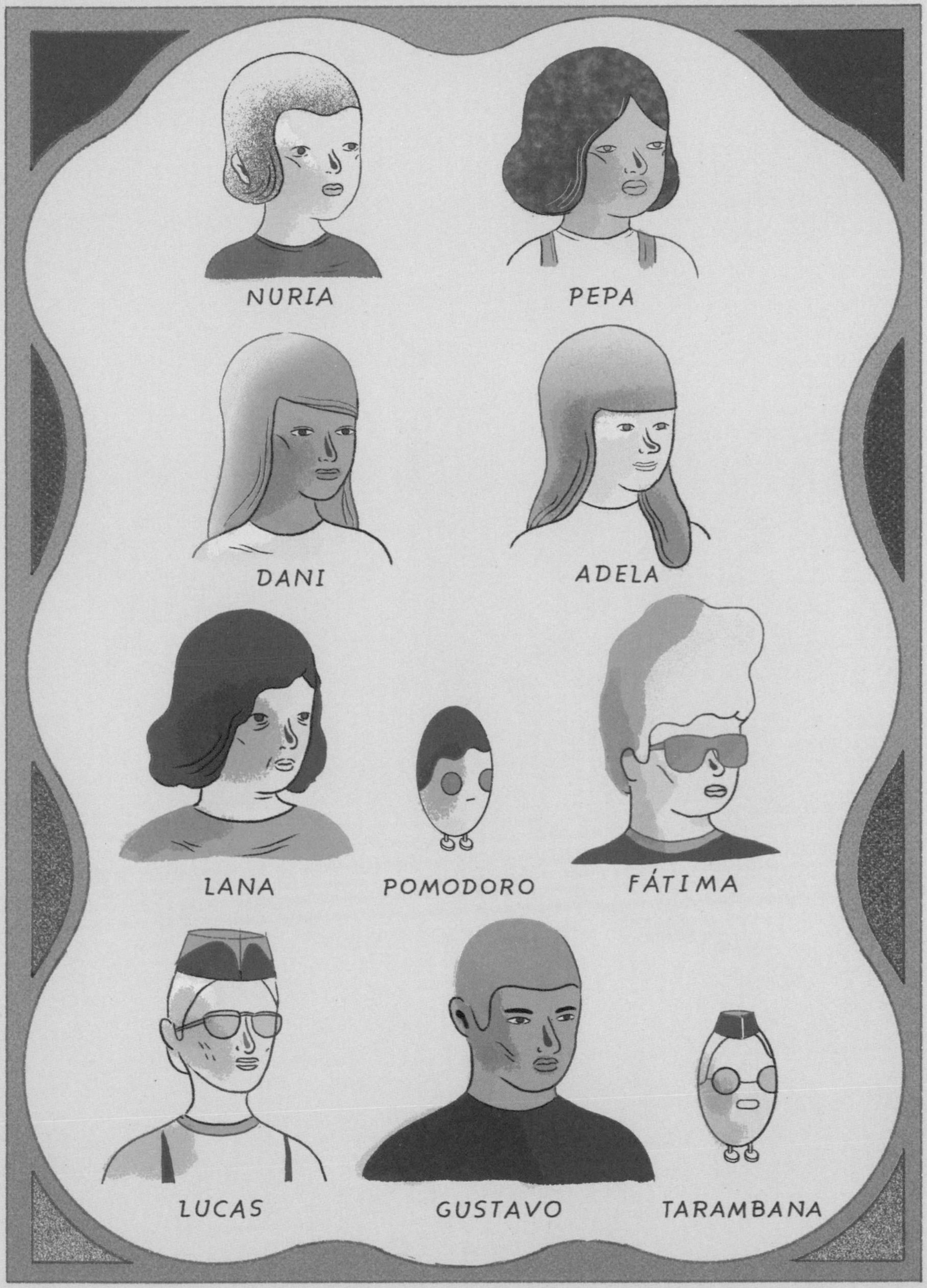
NURIA
PEPA
DANI
ADELA
LANA
POMODORO
FÁTIMA
LUCAS
GUSTAVO
TARAMBANA

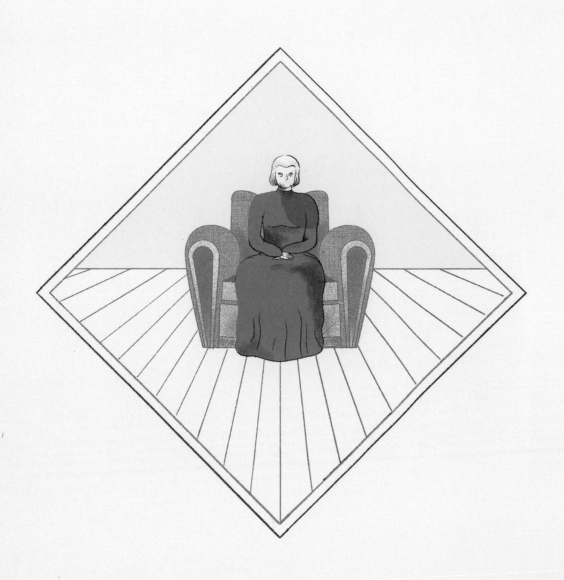

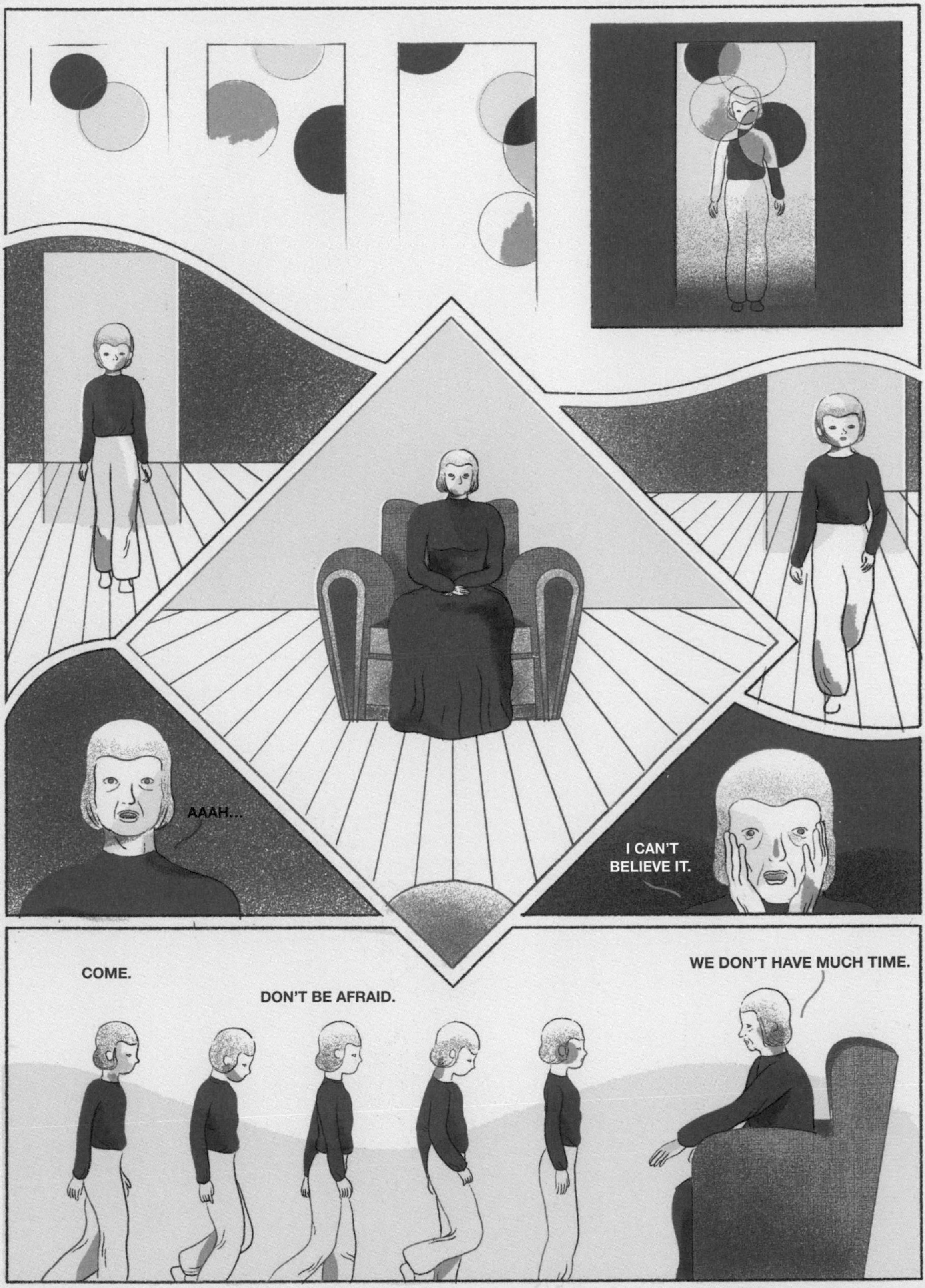
AAAH...
I CAN'T
BELIEVE IT.
COME.
DON'T BE AFRAID.
WE DON'T HAVE MUCH TIME.

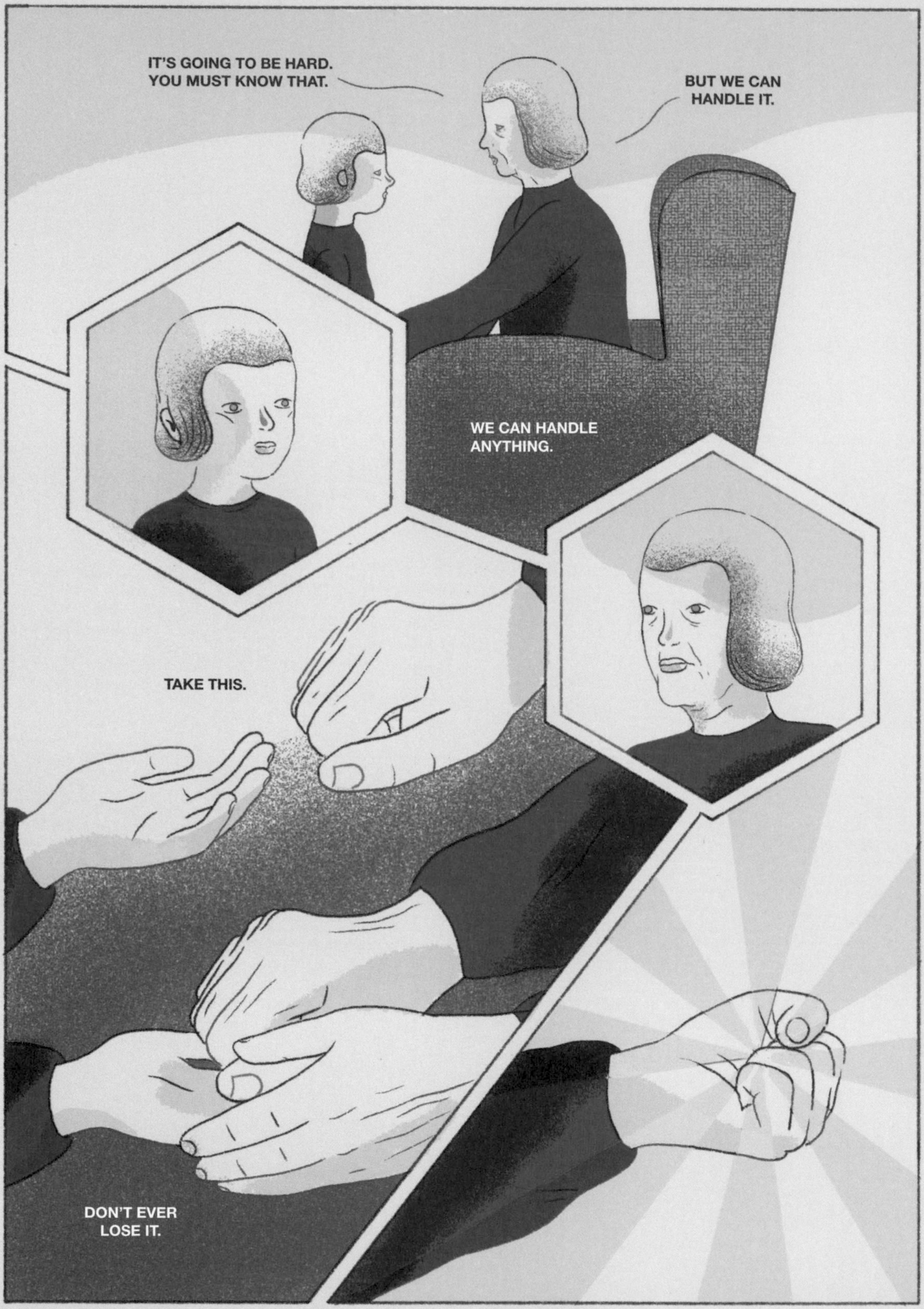
IT'S GOING TO BE HARD. YOU MUST KNOW THAT.
BUT WE CAN HANDLE IT.
WE CAN HANDLE ANYTHING.
TAKE THIS.
DON'T EVER LOSE IT.

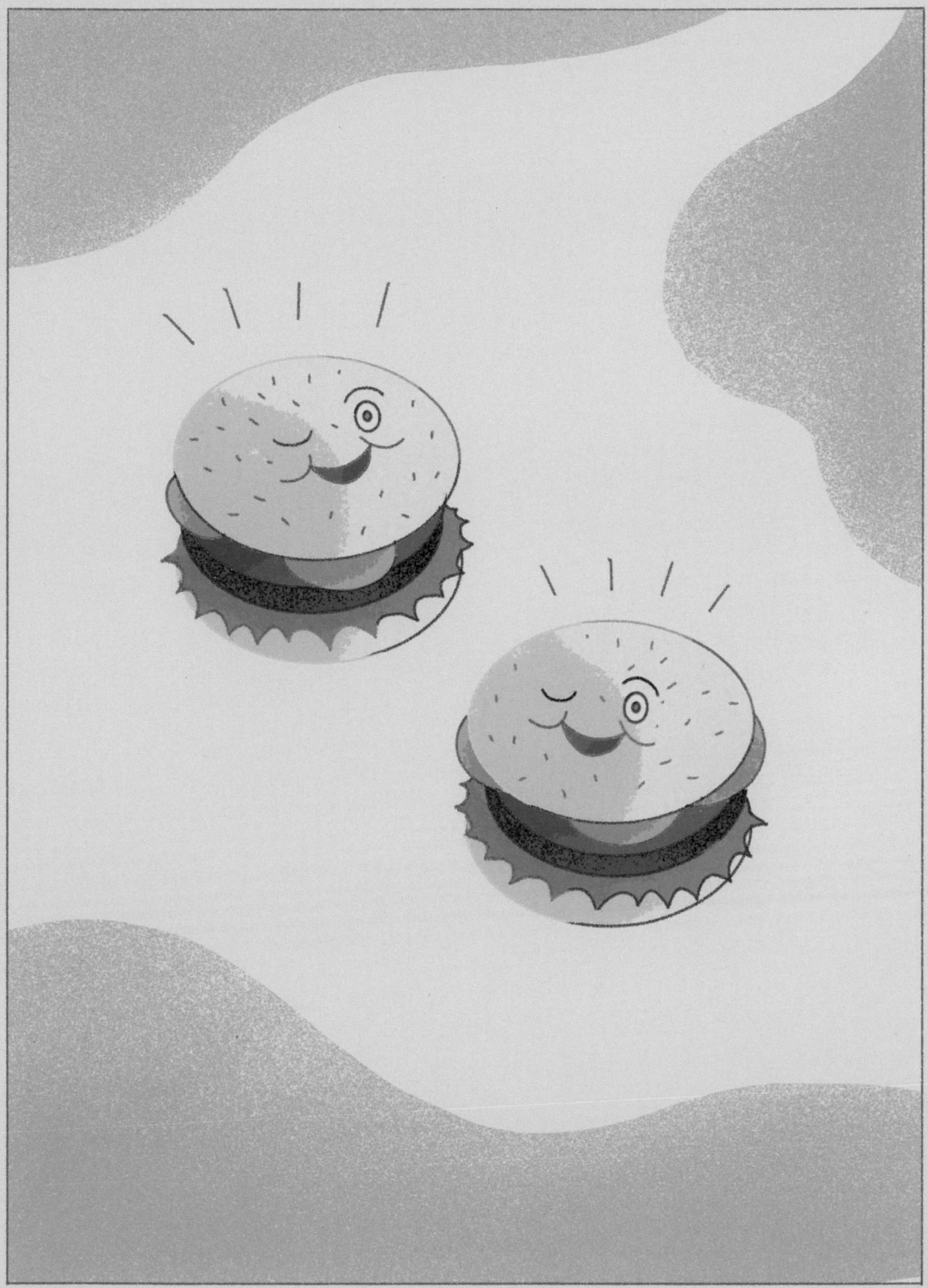

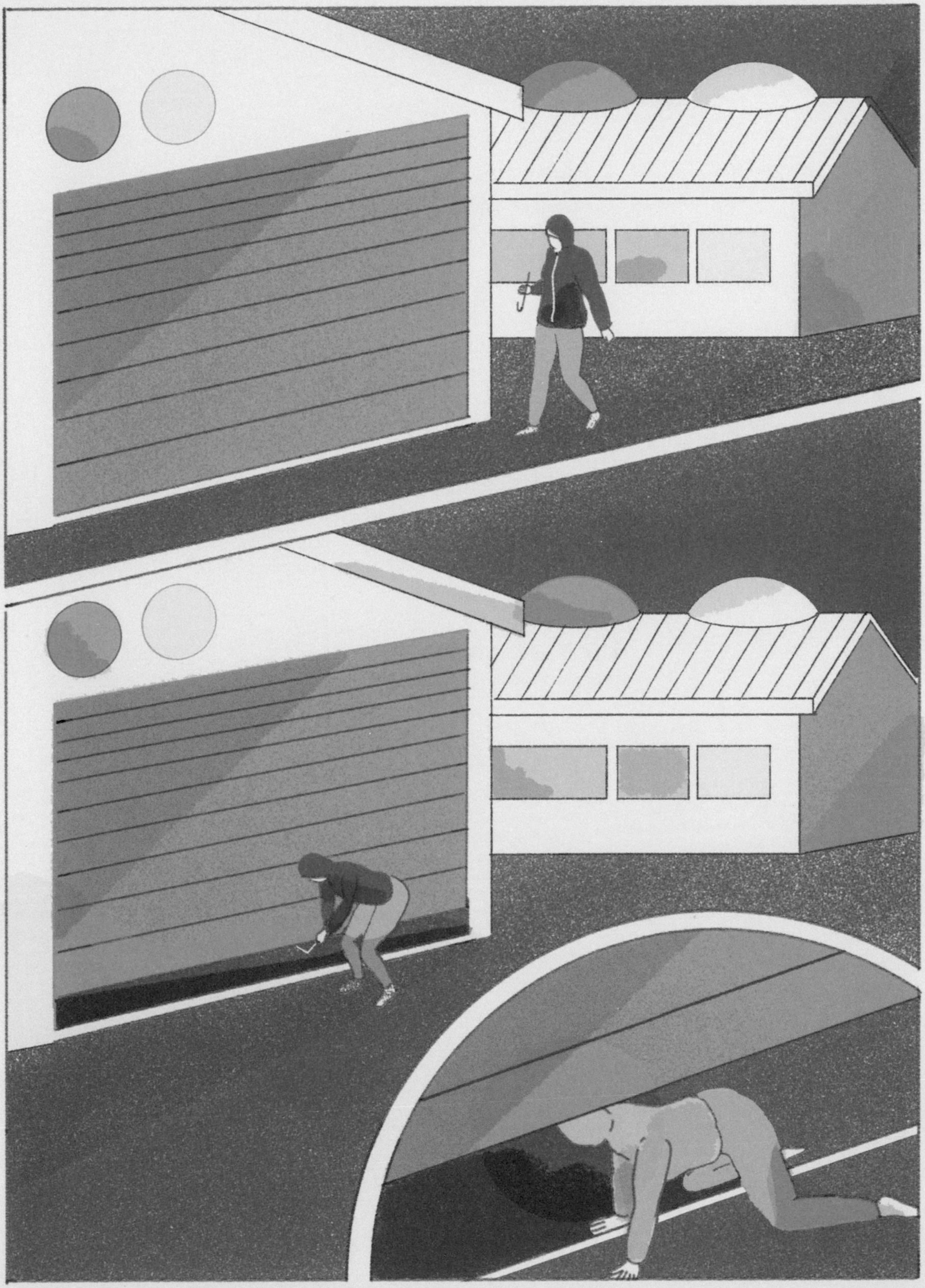

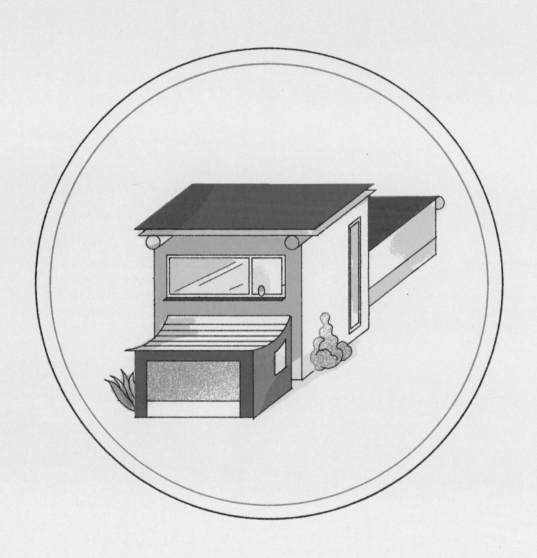

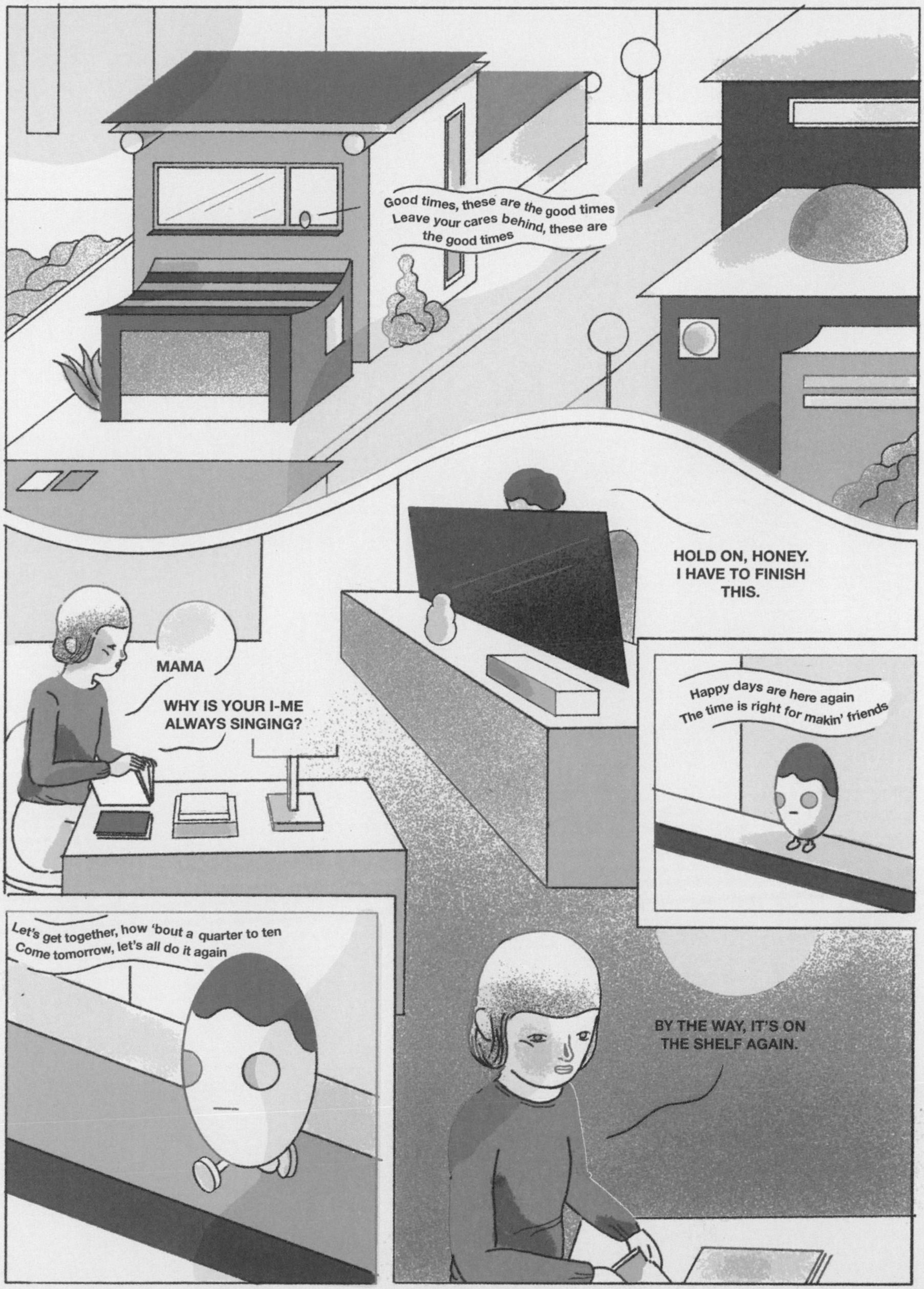
Good times, these are the good times
Leave your cares behind, these are the good times
HOLD ON, HONEY. I HAVE TO FINISH THIS.
MAMA
WHY IS YOUR I-ME ALWAYS SINGING?
Happy days are here again
The time is right for makin' friends
Let's get together, how 'bout a quarter to ten
Come tomorrow, let's all do it again
BY THE WAY, IT'S ON THE SHELF AGAIN.

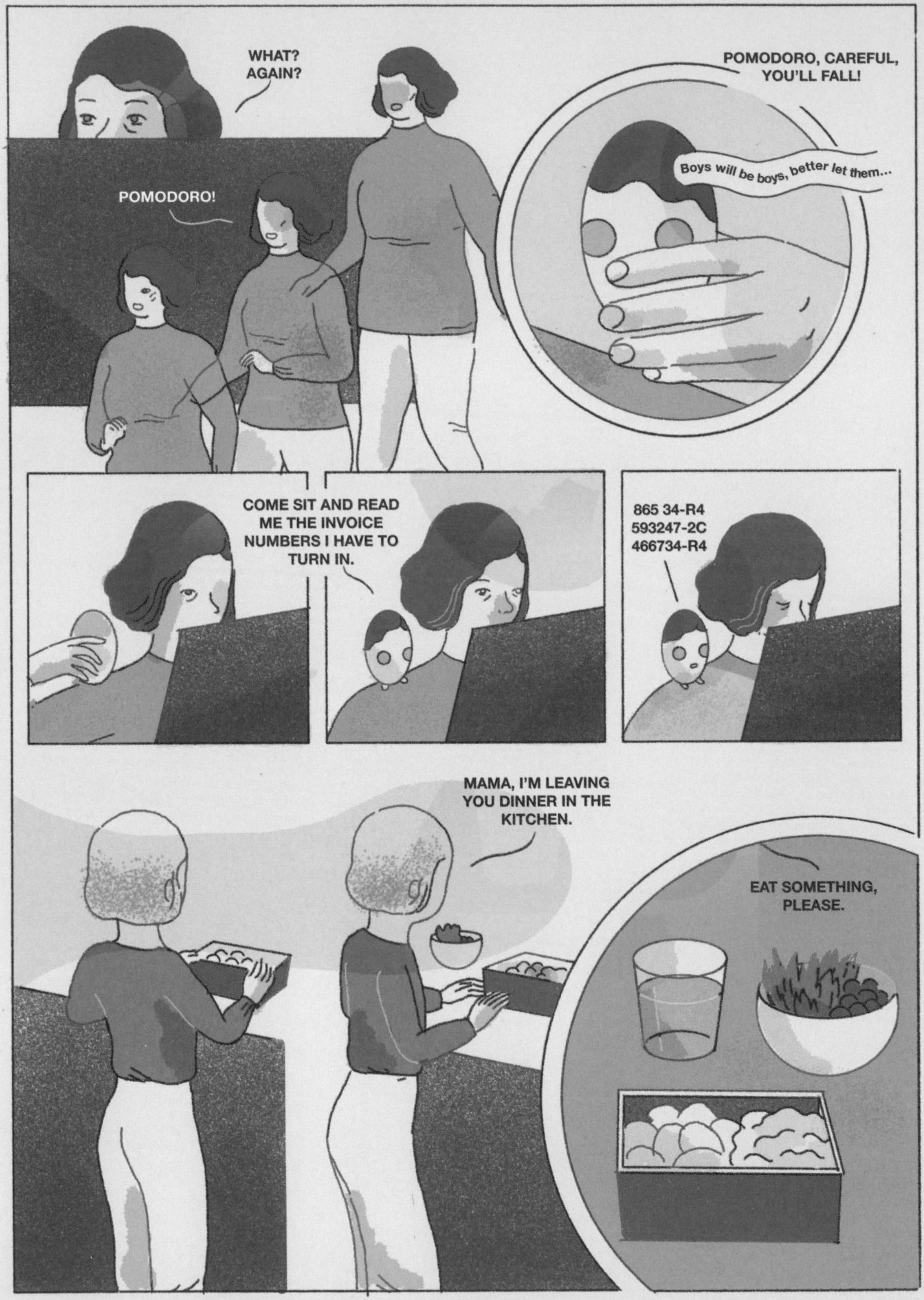
WHAT? AGAIN?
POMODORO!
POMODORO, CAREFUL, YOU'LL FALL!
Boys will be boys, better let them...
COME SIT AND READ ME THE INVOICE NUMBERS I HAVE TO TURN IN.
865 34-R4
593247-2C
466734-R4
MAMA, I'M LEAVING YOU DINNER IN THE KITCHEN.
EAT SOMETHING, PLEASE.

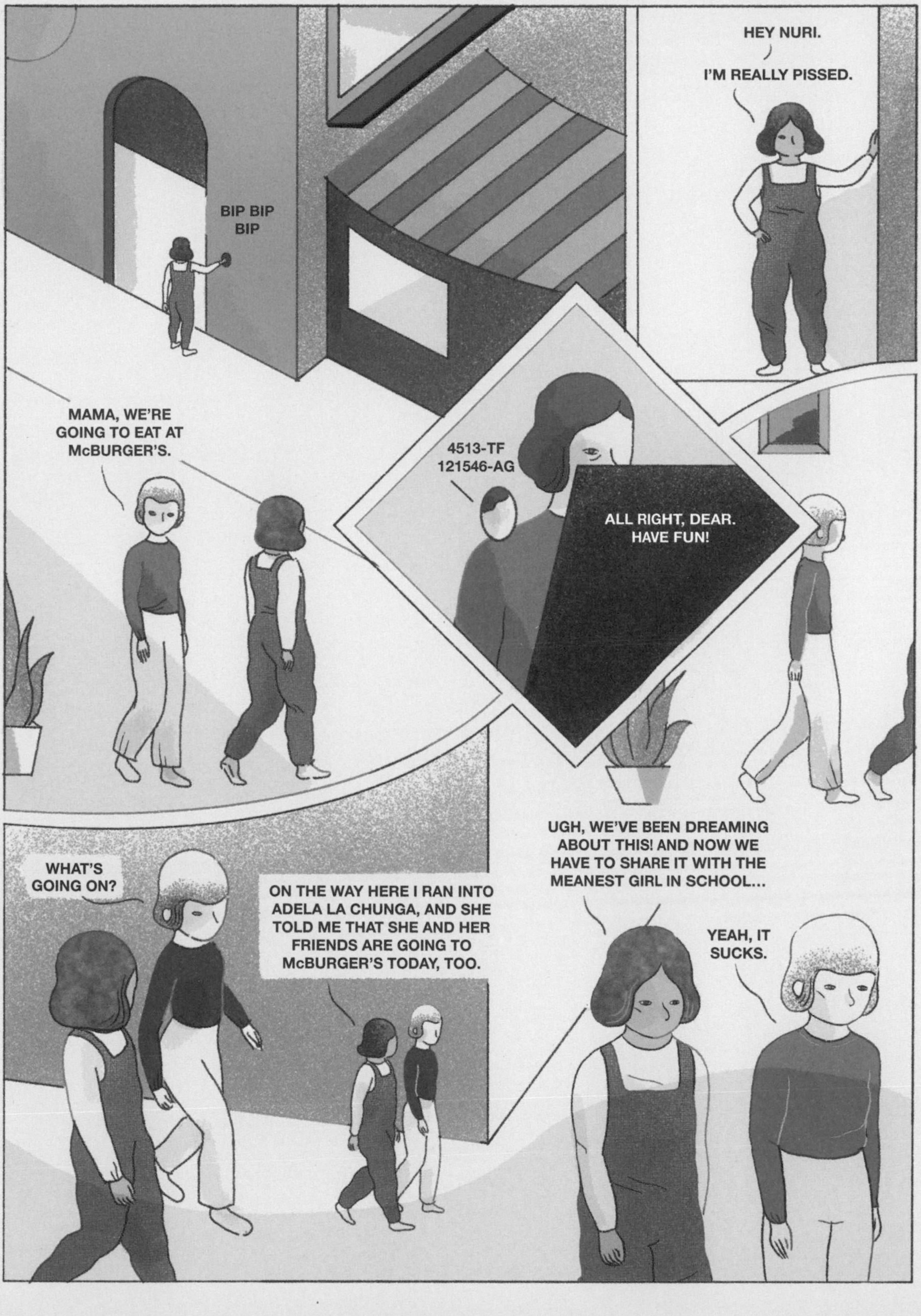
BIP BIP BIP
HEY NURI.
I'M REALLY PISSED.
MAMA, WE'RE GOING TO EAT AT McBURGER'S.
4513-TF 121546-AG
ALL RIGHT, DEAR. HAVE FUN!
WHAT'S GOING ON?
ON THE WAY HERE I RAN INTO ADELA LA CHUNGA, AND SHE TOLD ME THAT SHE AND HER FRIENDS ARE GOING TO McBURGER'S TODAY, TOO.
UGH, WE'VE BEEN DREAMING ABOUT THIS! AND NOW WE HAVE TO SHARE IT WITH THE MEANEST GIRL IN SCHOOL...
YEAH, IT SUCKS.

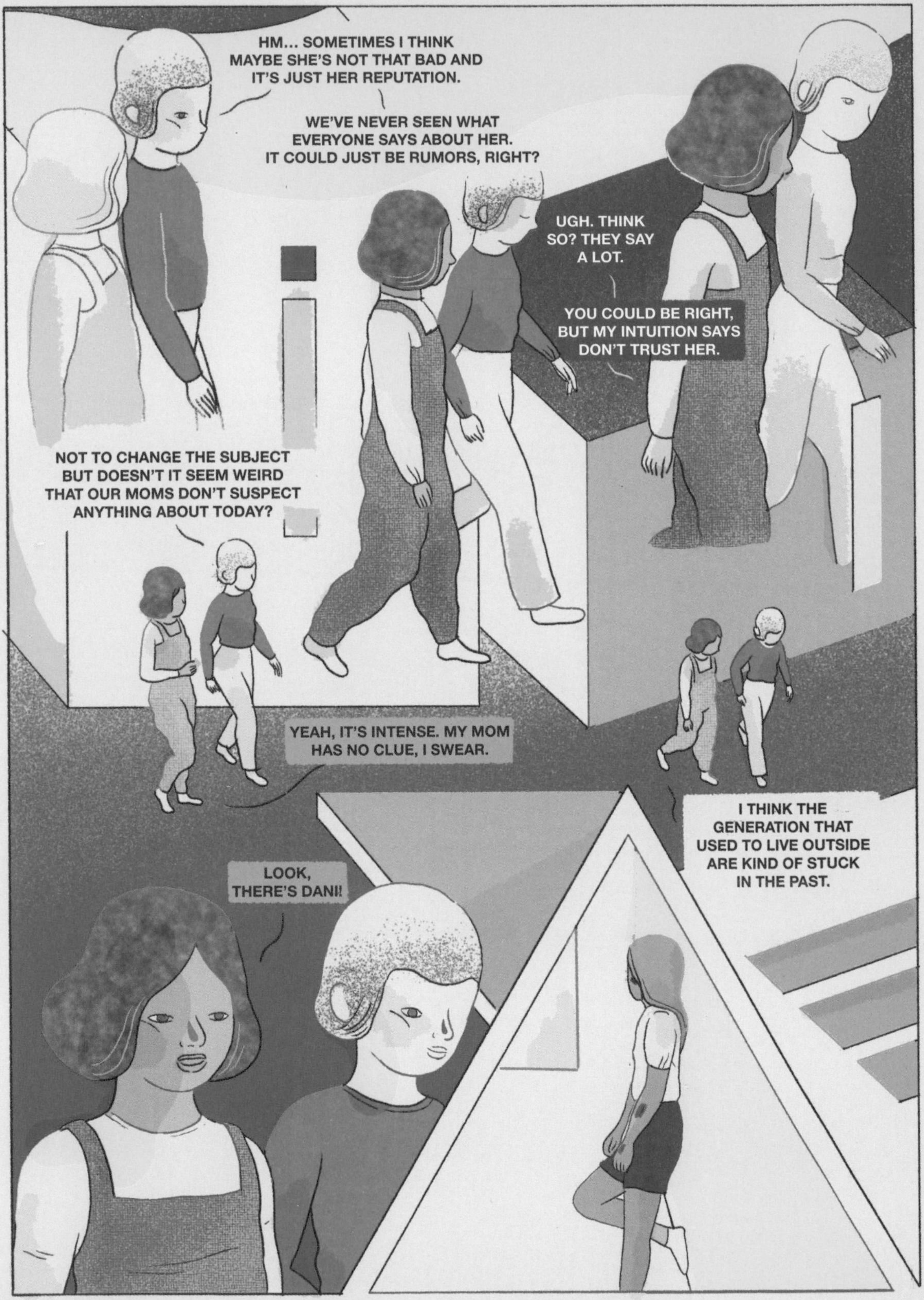
HM... SOMETIMES I THINK MAYBE SHE'S NOT THAT BAD AND IT'S JUST HER REPUTATION.
WE'VE NEVER SEEN WHAT EVERYONE SAYS ABOUT HER. IT COULD JUST BE RUMORS, RIGHT?
UGH. THINK SO? THEY SAY A LOT.
YOU COULD BE RIGHT, BUT MY INTUITION SAYS DON'T TRUST HER.
NOT TO CHANGE THE SUBJECT BUT DOESN'T IT SEEM WEIRD THAT OUR MOMS DON'T SUSPECT ANYTHING ABOUT TODAY?
YEAH, IT'S INTENSE. MY MOM HAS NO CLUE, I SWEAR.
I THINK THE GENERATION THAT USED TO LIVE OUTSIDE ARE KIND OF STUCK IN THE PAST.
LOOK, THERE'S DANI!

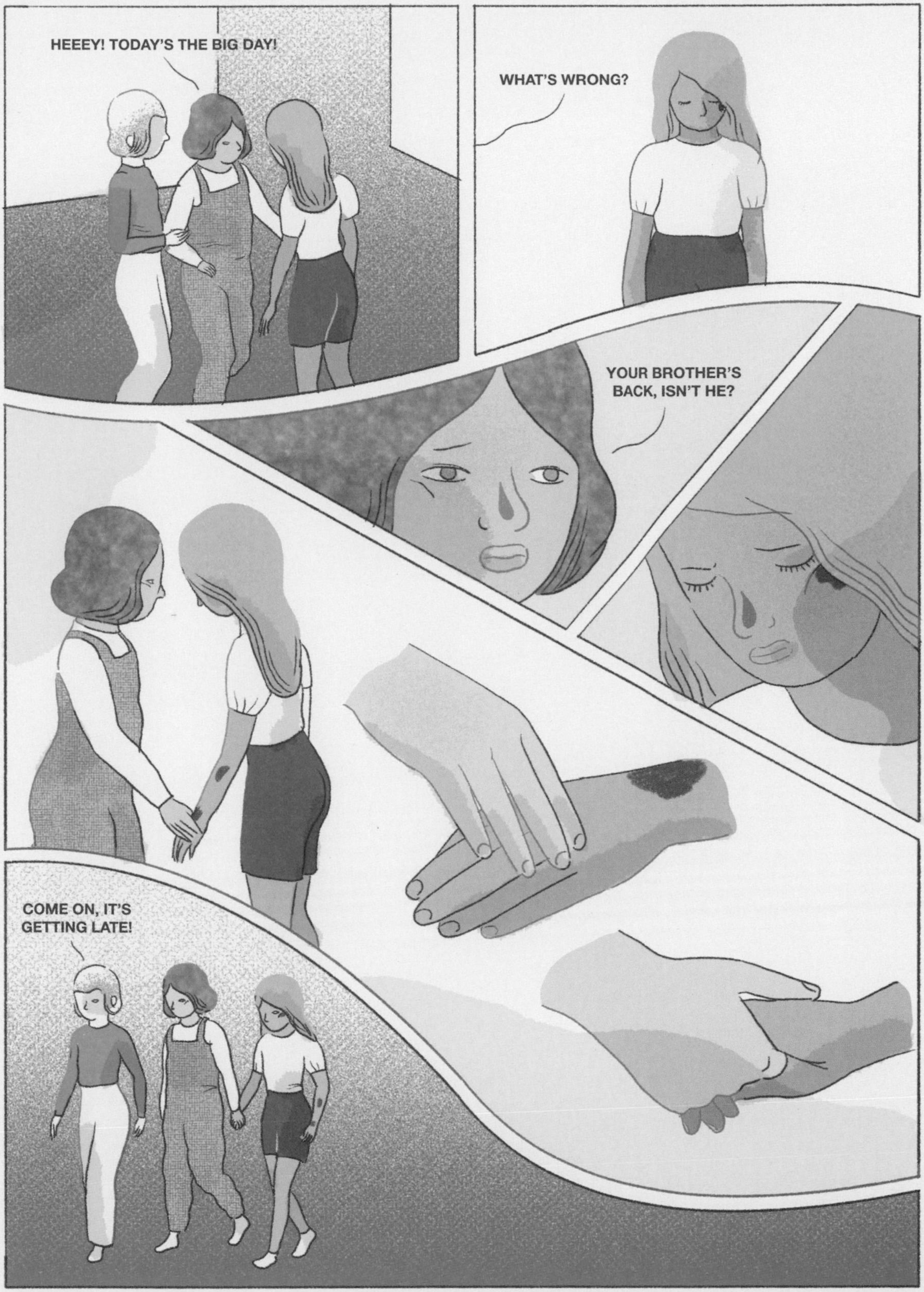
HEEEY! TODAY'S THE BIG DAY!
WHAT'S WRONG?
YOUR BROTHER'S BACK, ISN'T HE?
COME ON, IT'S GETTING LATE!

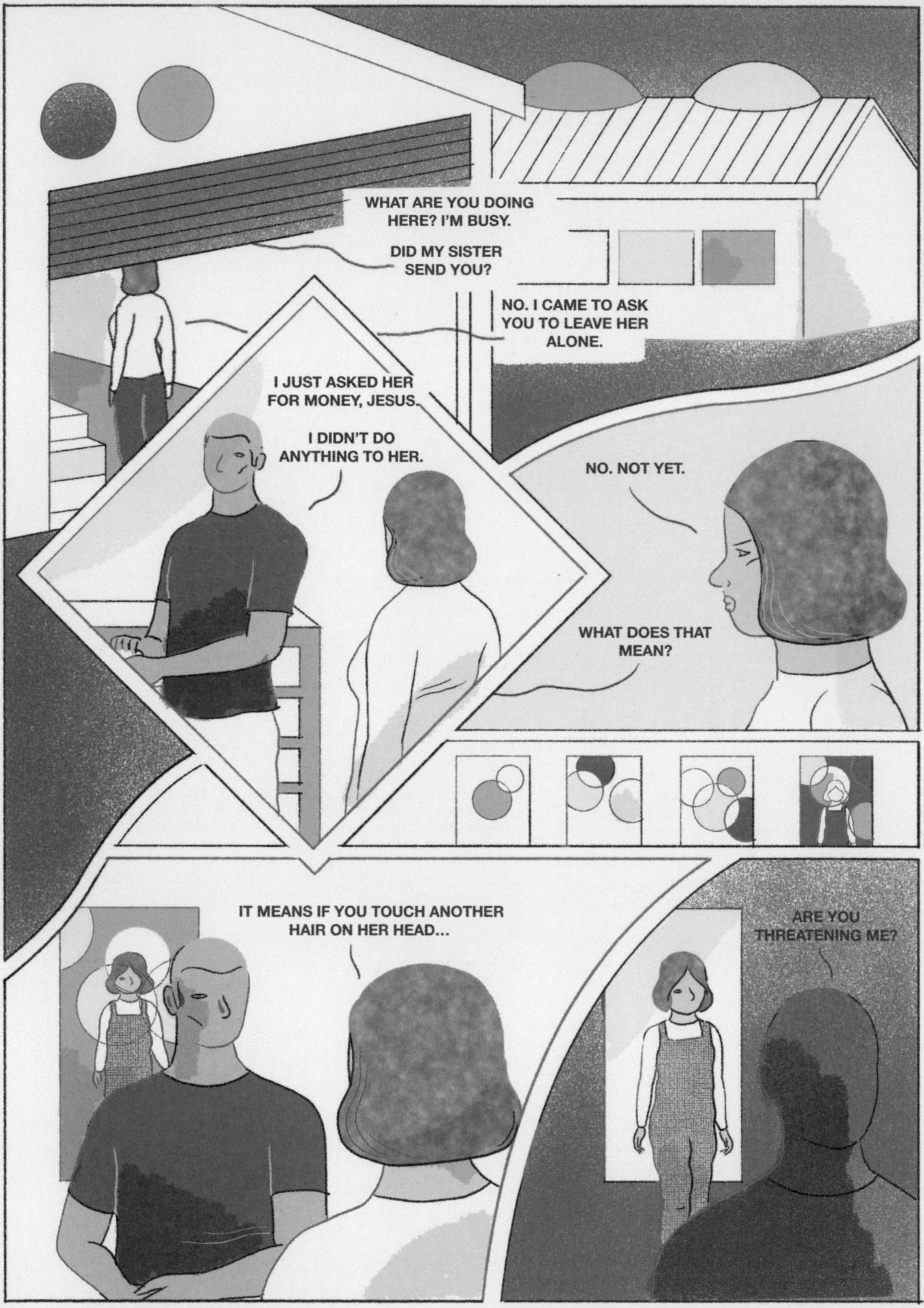
WHAT ARE YOU DOING HERE? I'M BUSY.
DID MY SISTER SEND YOU?
NO. I CAME TO ASK YOU TO LEAVE HER ALONE.
I JUST ASKED HER FOR MONEY, JESUS.
I DIDN'T DO ANYTHING TO HER.
NO. NOT YET.
WHAT DOES THAT MEAN?
IT MEANS IF YOU TOUCH ANOTHER HAIR ON HER HEAD...
ARE YOU THREATENING ME?

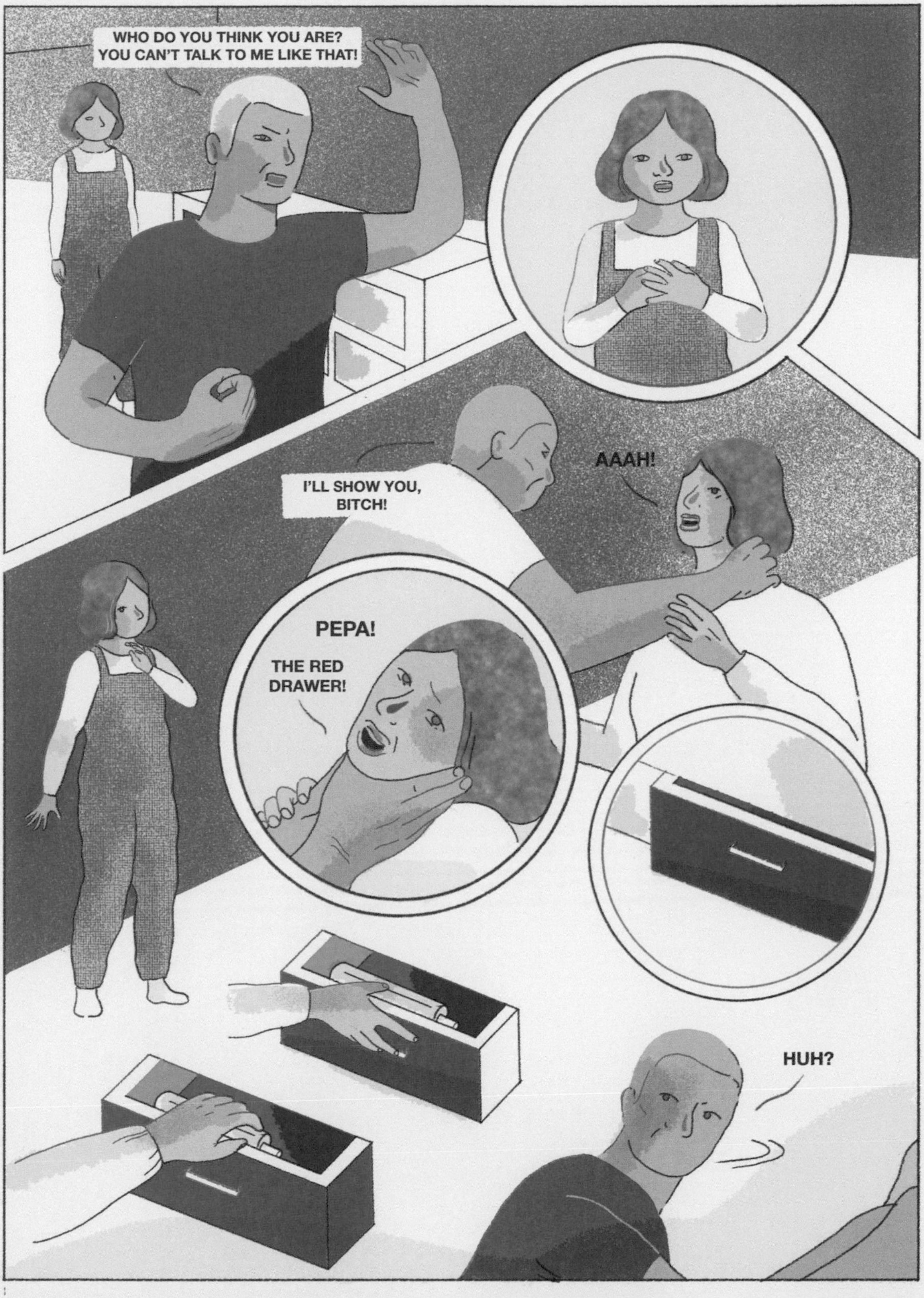
WHO DO YOU THINK YOU ARE?
YOU CAN'T TALK TO ME LIKE THAT!
I'LL SHOW YOU, BITCH!
AAAH!
PEPA!
THE RED DRAWER!
HUH?

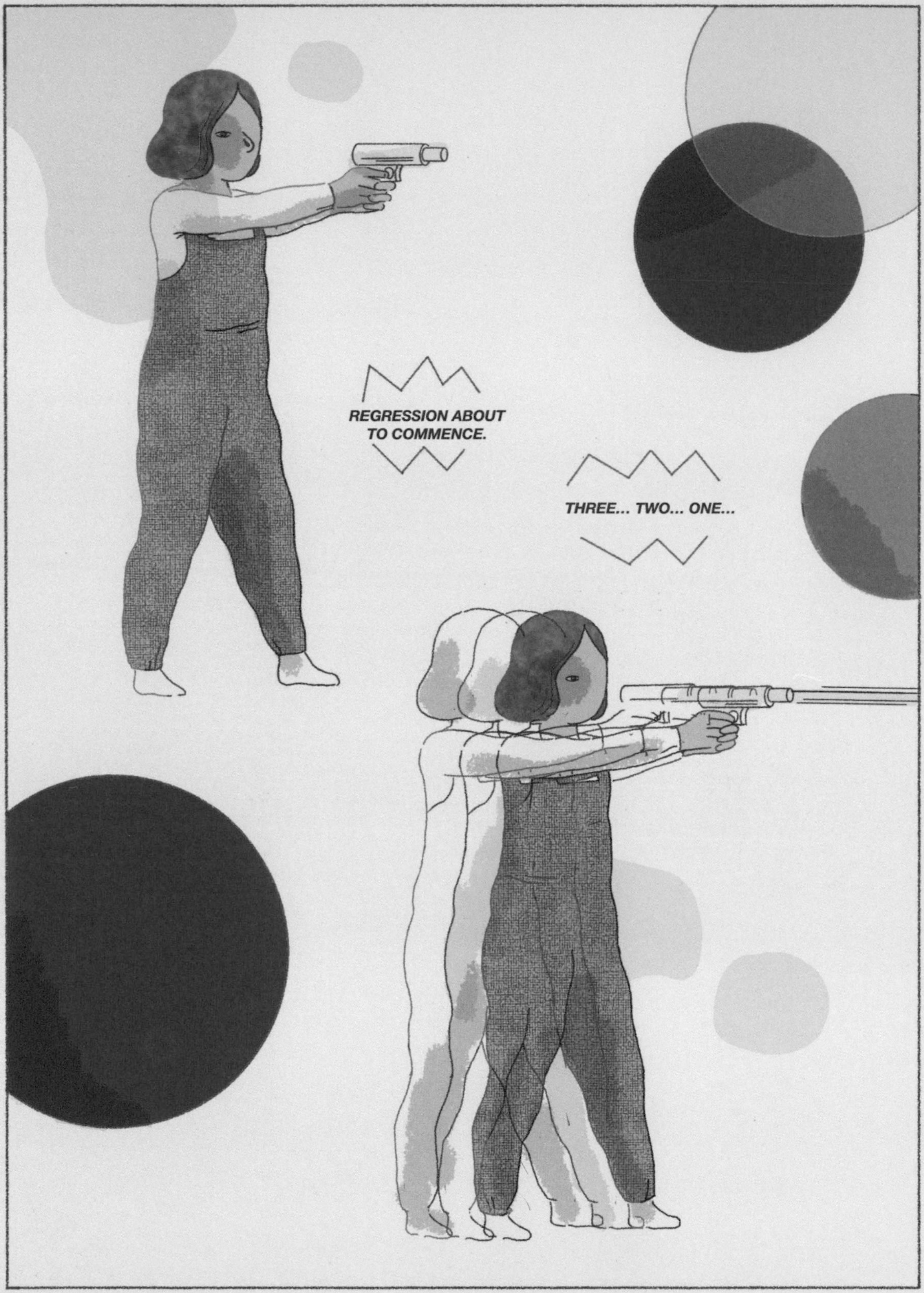
REGRESSION ABOUT TO COMMENCE.
THREE... TWO... ONE...

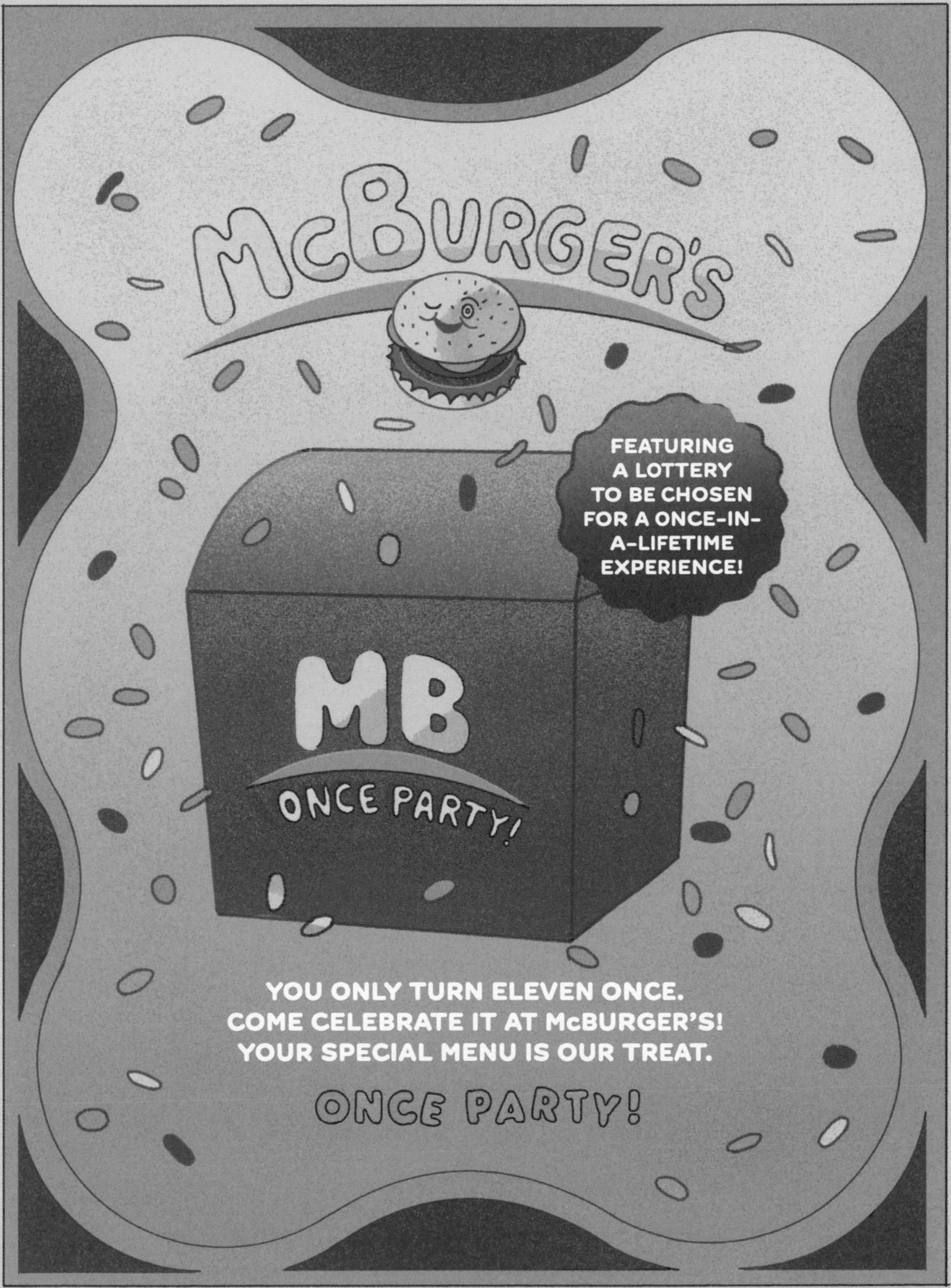
McBURGER'S
FEATURING A LOTTERY TO BE CHOSEN FOR A ONCE-IN-A-LIFETIME EXPERIENCE!
MB
ONCE PARTY!
YOU ONLY TURN ELEVEN ONCE.
COME CELEBRATE IT AT McBURGER'S!
YOUR SPECIAL MENU IS OUR TREAT.
ONCE PARTY!

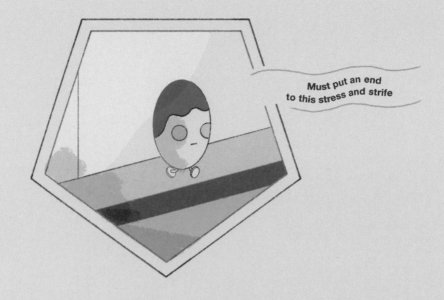

Must put an end
to this stress and strife

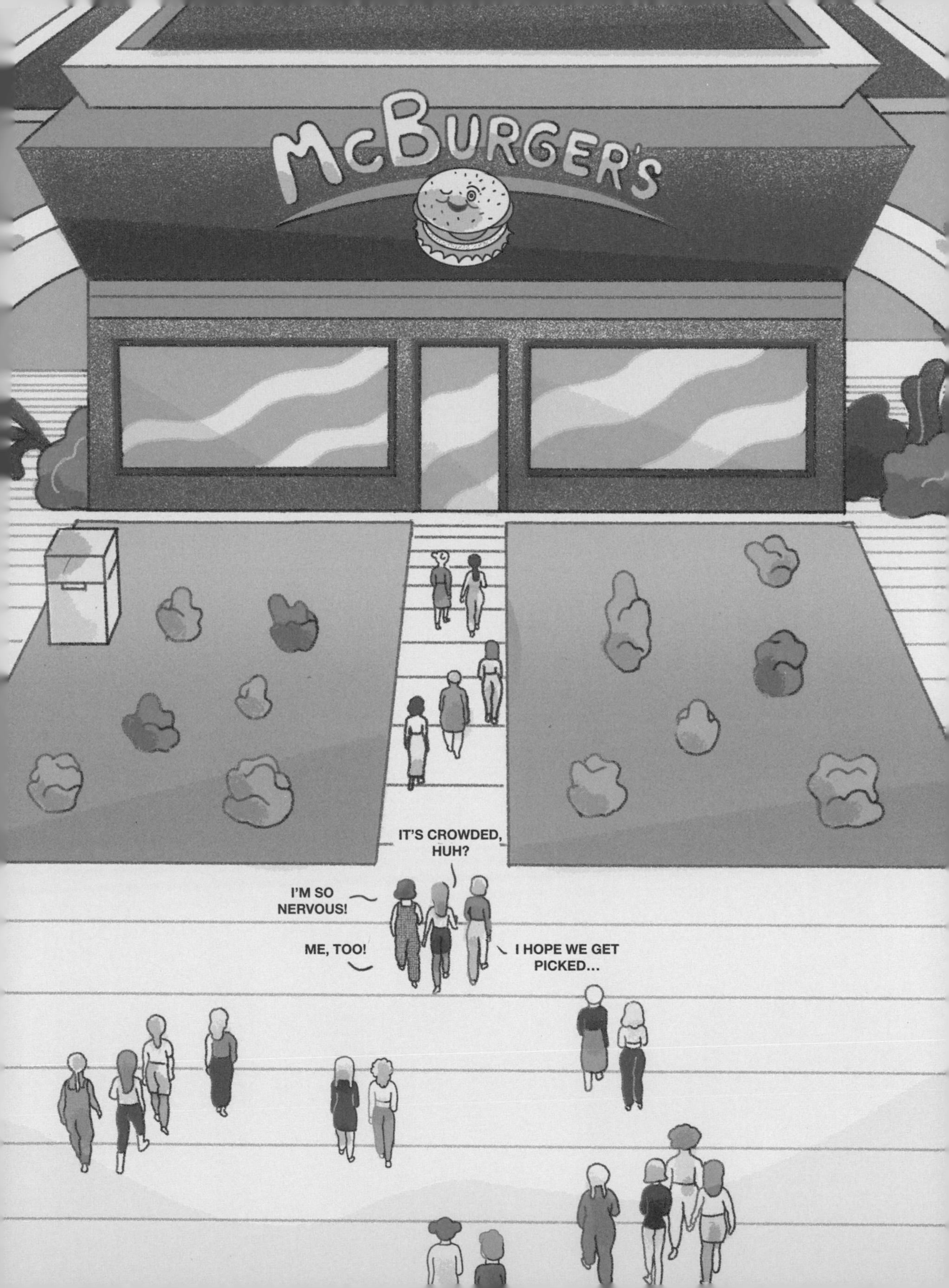
McBURGER'S
IT'S CROWDED, HUH?
I'M SO NERVOUS!
ME, TOO!
I HOPE WE GET PICKED...

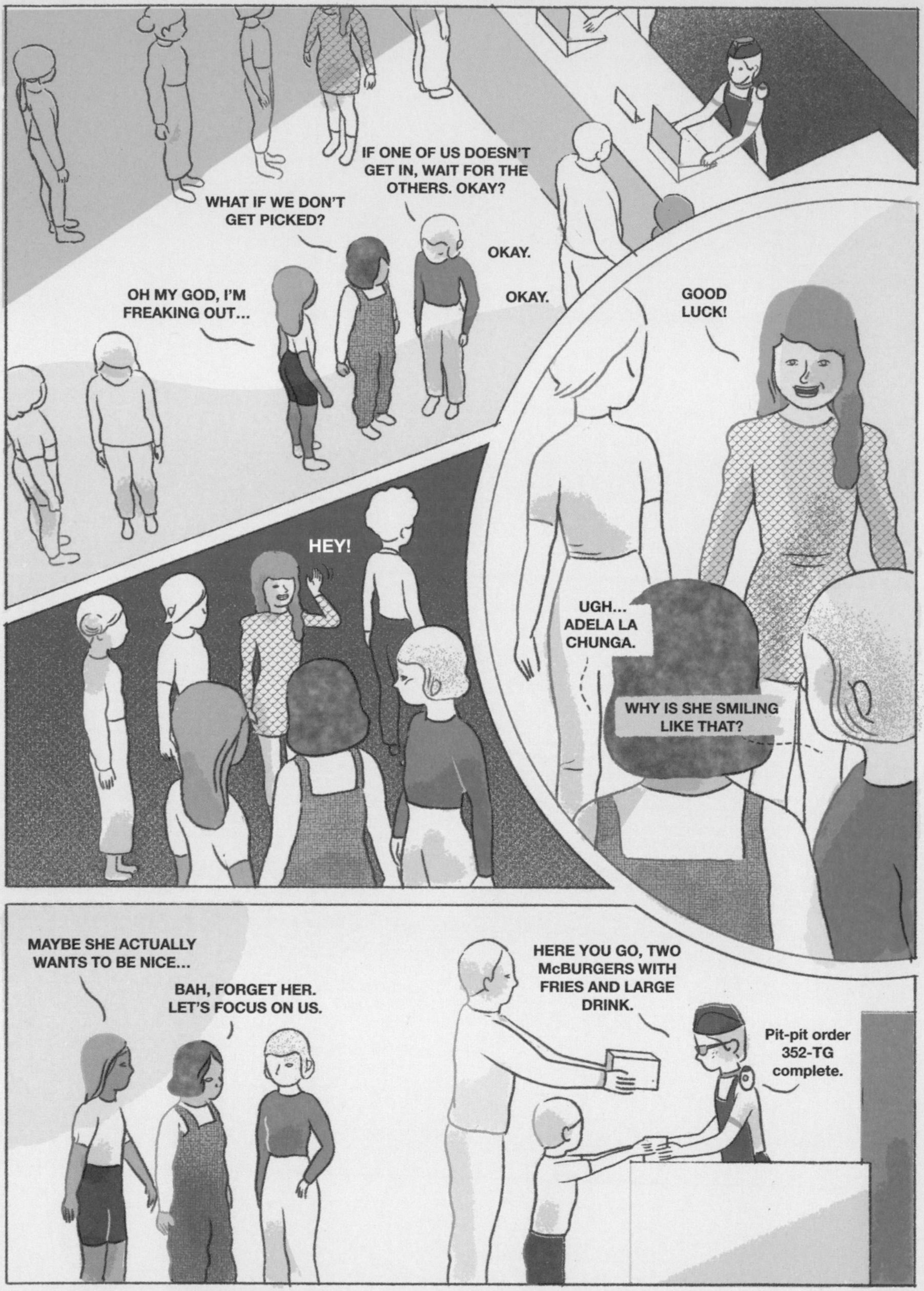
IF ONE OF US DOESN'T GET IN, WAIT FOR THE OTHERS. OKAY?
WHAT IF WE DON'T GET PICKED?
OKAY.
OKAY.
OH MY GOD, I'M FREAKING OUT...
GOOD LUCK!
HEY!
UGH... ADELA LA CHUNGA.
WHY IS SHE SMILING LIKE THAT?
MAYBE SHE ACTUALLY WANTS TO BE NICE...
BAH, FORGET HER. LET'S FOCUS ON US.
HERE YOU GO, TWO McBURGERS WITH FRIES AND LARGE DRINK.
Pit-pit order 352-TG complete.

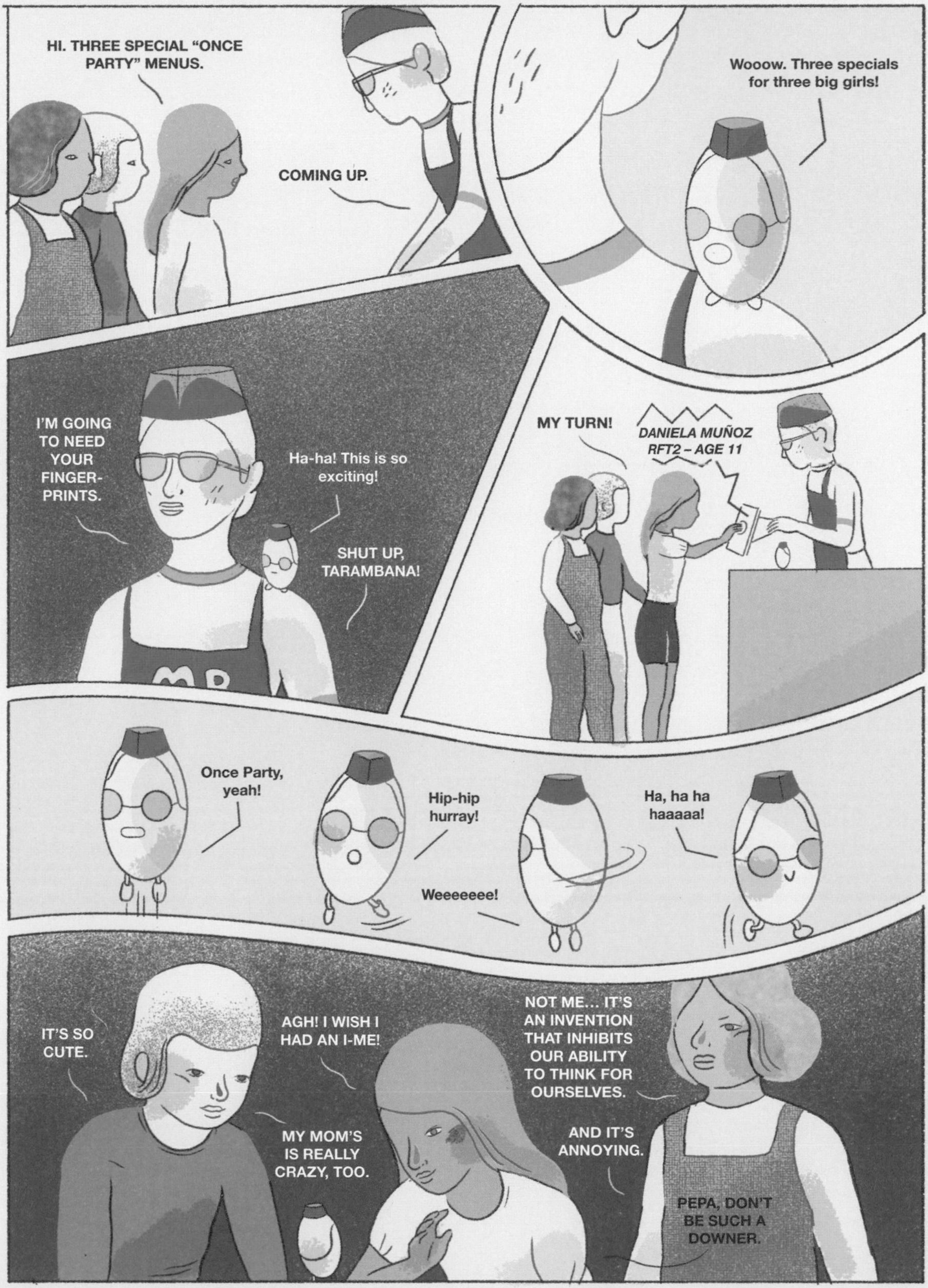
HI. THREE SPECIAL "ONCE PARTY" MENUS.
COMING UP.
Wooow. Three specials for three big girls!
I'M GOING TO NEED YOUR FINGER-PRINTS.
Ha-ha! This is so exciting!
SHUT UP, TARAMBANA!
MY TURN!
DANIELA MUÑOZ RFT2 – AGE 11
Once Party, yeah!
Hip-hip hurray!
Weeeeeee!
Ha, ha ha haaaaa!
IT'S SO CUTE.
AGH! I WISH I HAD AN I-ME!
MY MOM'S IS REALLY CRAZY, TOO.
NOT ME... IT'S AN INVENTION THAT INHIBITS OUR ABILITY TO THINK FOR OURSELVES.
AND IT'S ANNOYING.
PEPA, DON'T BE SUCH A DOWNER.

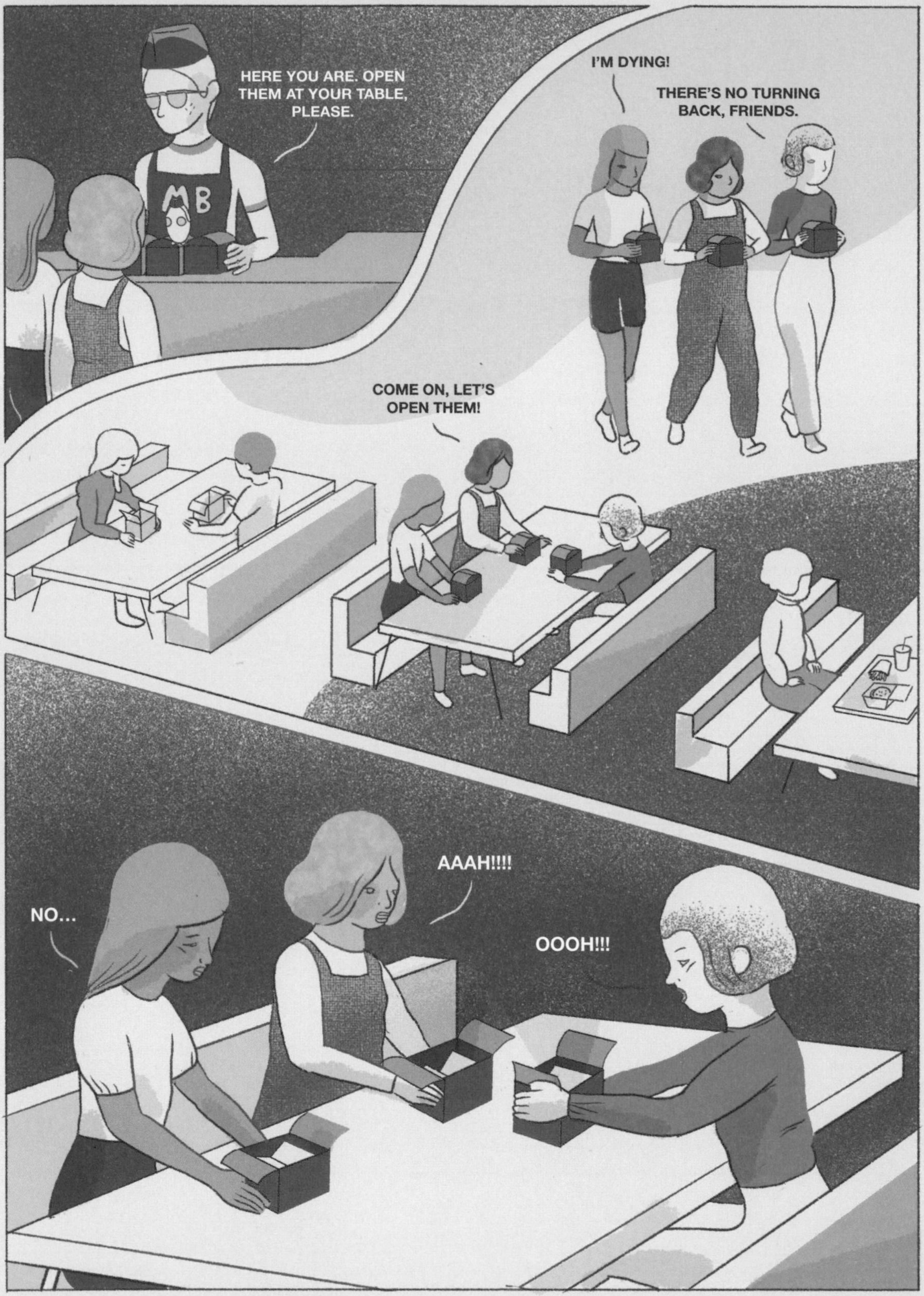
HERE YOU ARE. OPEN THEM AT YOUR TABLE, PLEASE.
MB
I'M DYING!
THERE'S NO TURNING BACK, FRIENDS.
COME ON, LET'S OPEN THEM!
NO...
AAAH!!!!
OOOH!!!

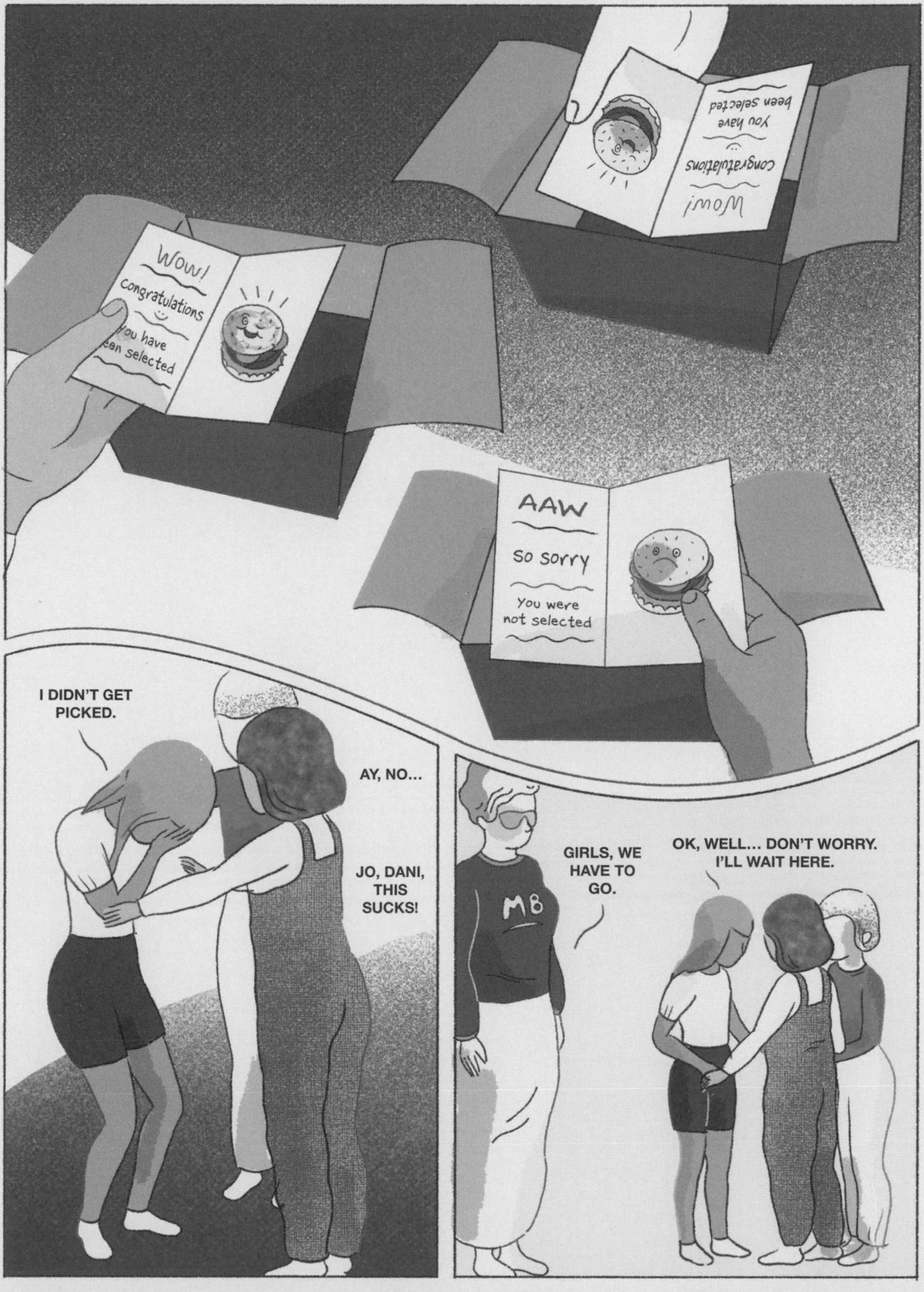
Wow!
Congratulations
You have been selected
Wow!
Congratulations
You have been selected
AAW
So sorry
You were not selected
I DIDN'T GET PICKED.
AY, NO...
JO, DANI, THIS SUCKS!
GIRLS, WE HAVE TO GO.
OK, WELL... DON'T WORRY. I'LL WAIT HERE.
MB

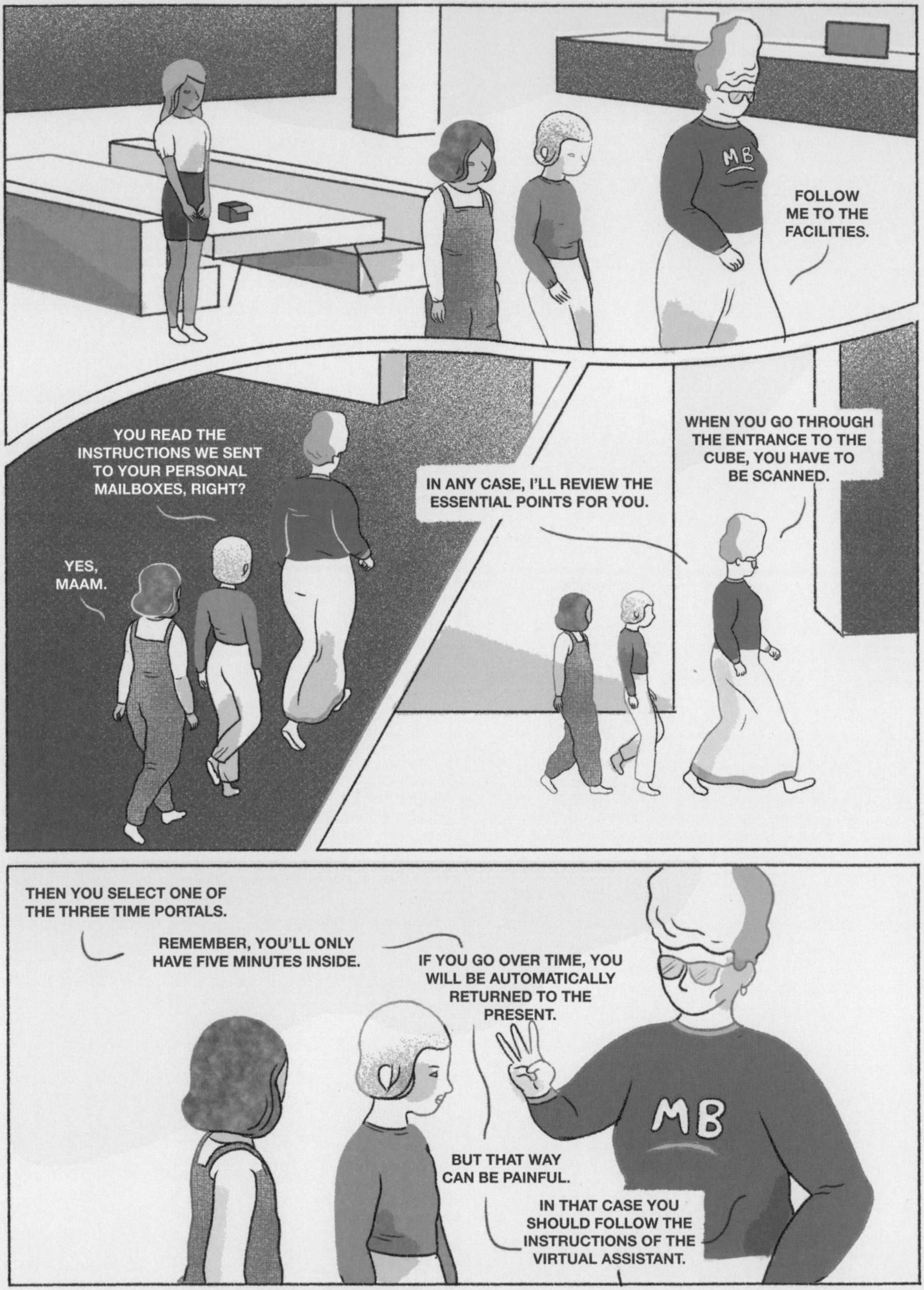

FOLLOW ME TO THE FACILITIES.
YOU READ THE INSTRUCTIONS WE SENT TO YOUR PERSONAL MAILBOXES, RIGHT?
YES, MAAM.
IN ANY CASE, I'LL REVIEW THE ESSENTIAL POINTS FOR YOU.
WHEN YOU GO THROUGH THE ENTRANCE TO THE CUBE, YOU HAVE TO BE SCANNED.
THEN YOU SELECT ONE OF THE THREE TIME PORTALS.
REMEMBER, YOU'LL ONLY HAVE FIVE MINUTES INSIDE.
IF YOU GO OVER TIME, YOU WILL BE AUTOMATICALLY RETURNED TO THE PRESENT.
BUT THAT WAY CAN BE PAINFUL.
IN THAT CASE YOU SHOULD FOLLOW THE INSTRUCTIONS OF THE VIRTUAL ASSISTANT.

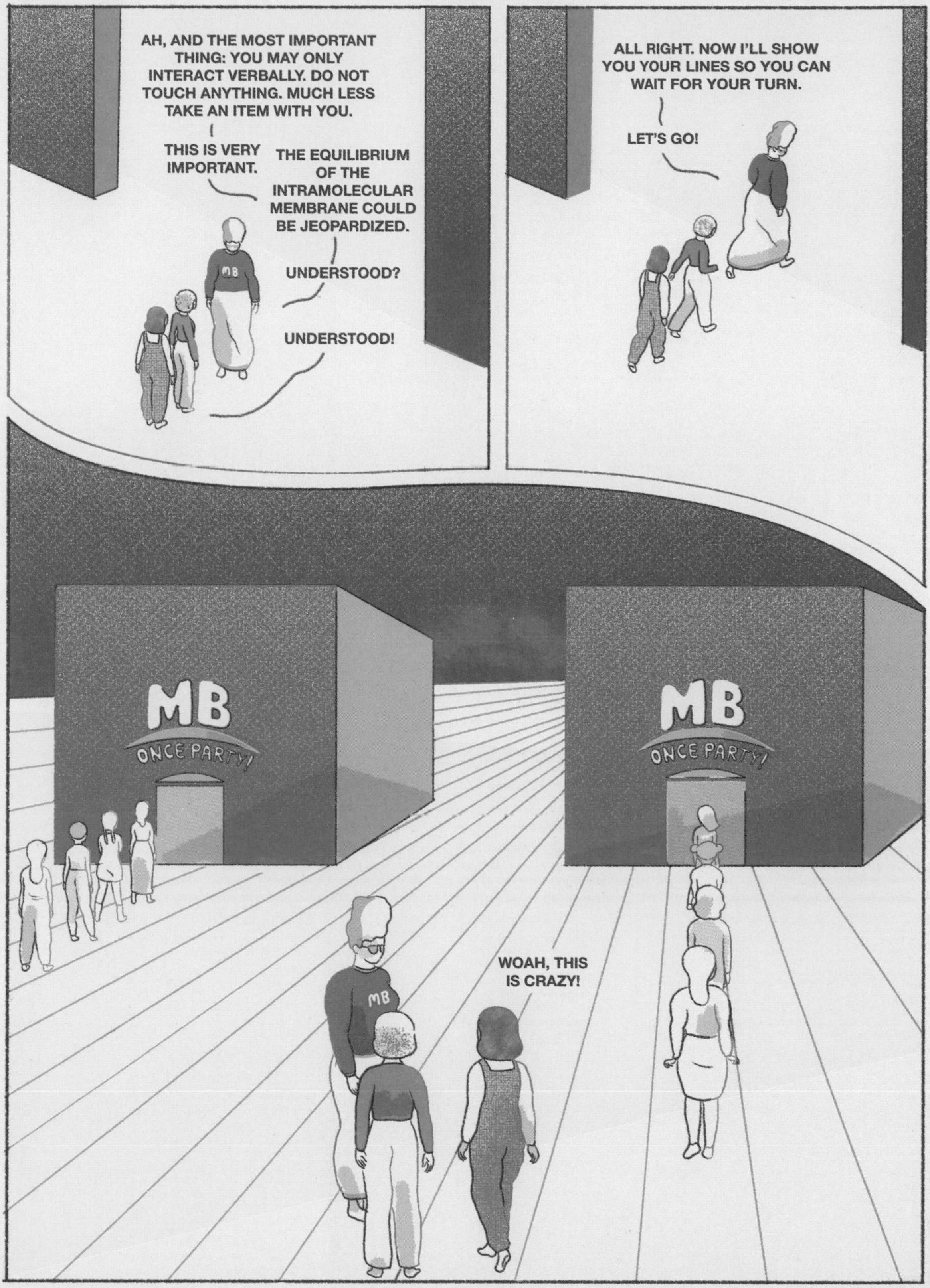
AH, AND THE MOST IMPORTANT THING: YOU MAY ONLY INTERACT VERBALLY. DO NOT TOUCH ANYTHING. MUCH LESS TAKE AN ITEM WITH YOU.
THIS IS VERY IMPORTANT.
THE EQUILIBRIUM OF THE INTRAMOLECULAR MEMBRANE COULD BE JEOPARDIZED.
UNDERSTOOD?
UNDERSTOOD!
MB
ALL RIGHT. NOW I'LL SHOW YOU YOUR LINES SO YOU CAN WAIT FOR YOUR TURN.
LET'S GO!
MB
ONCE PARTY!
MB
ONCE PARTY!
MB
WOAH, THIS IS CRAZY!

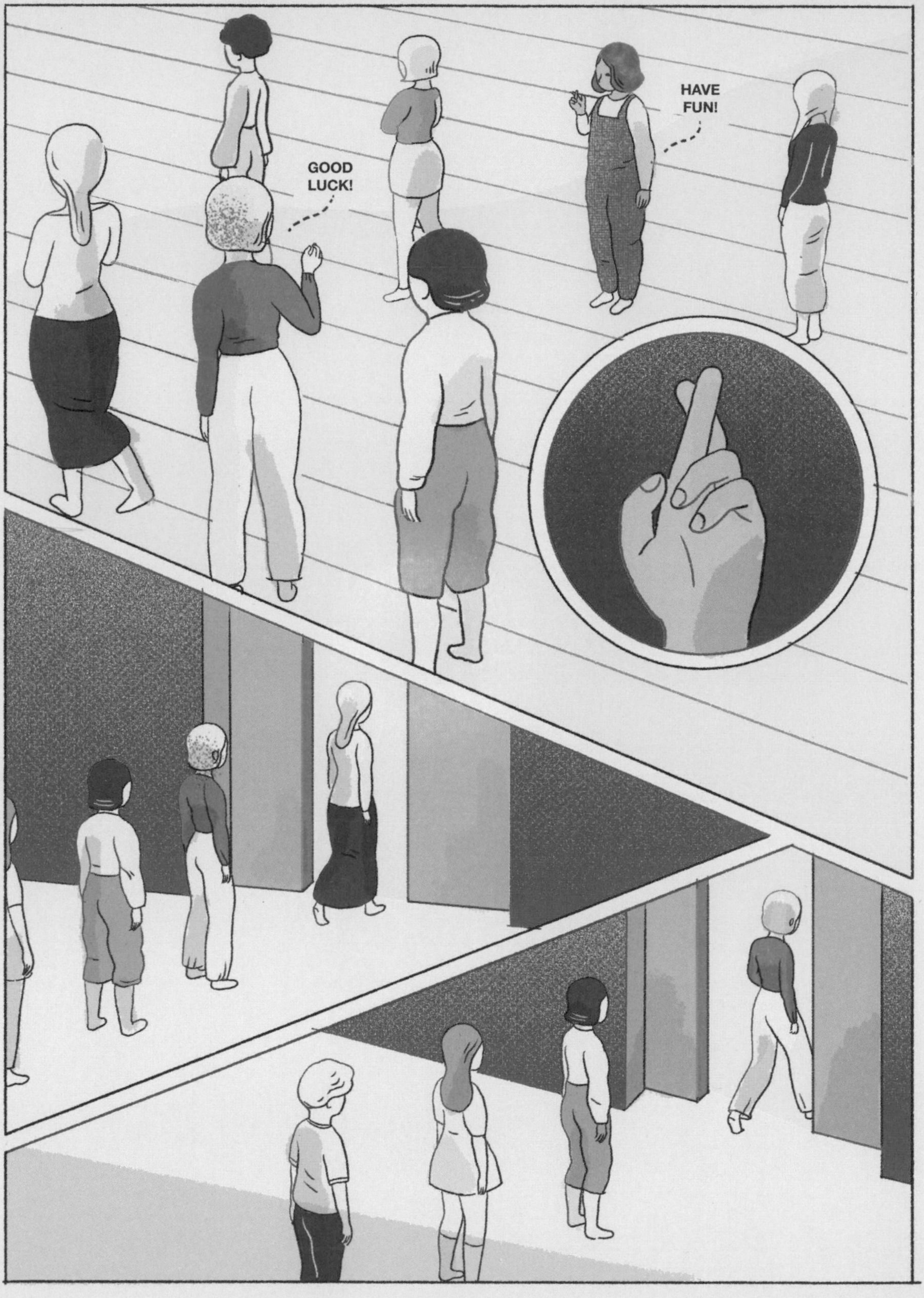
GOOD LUCK!
HAVE FUN!

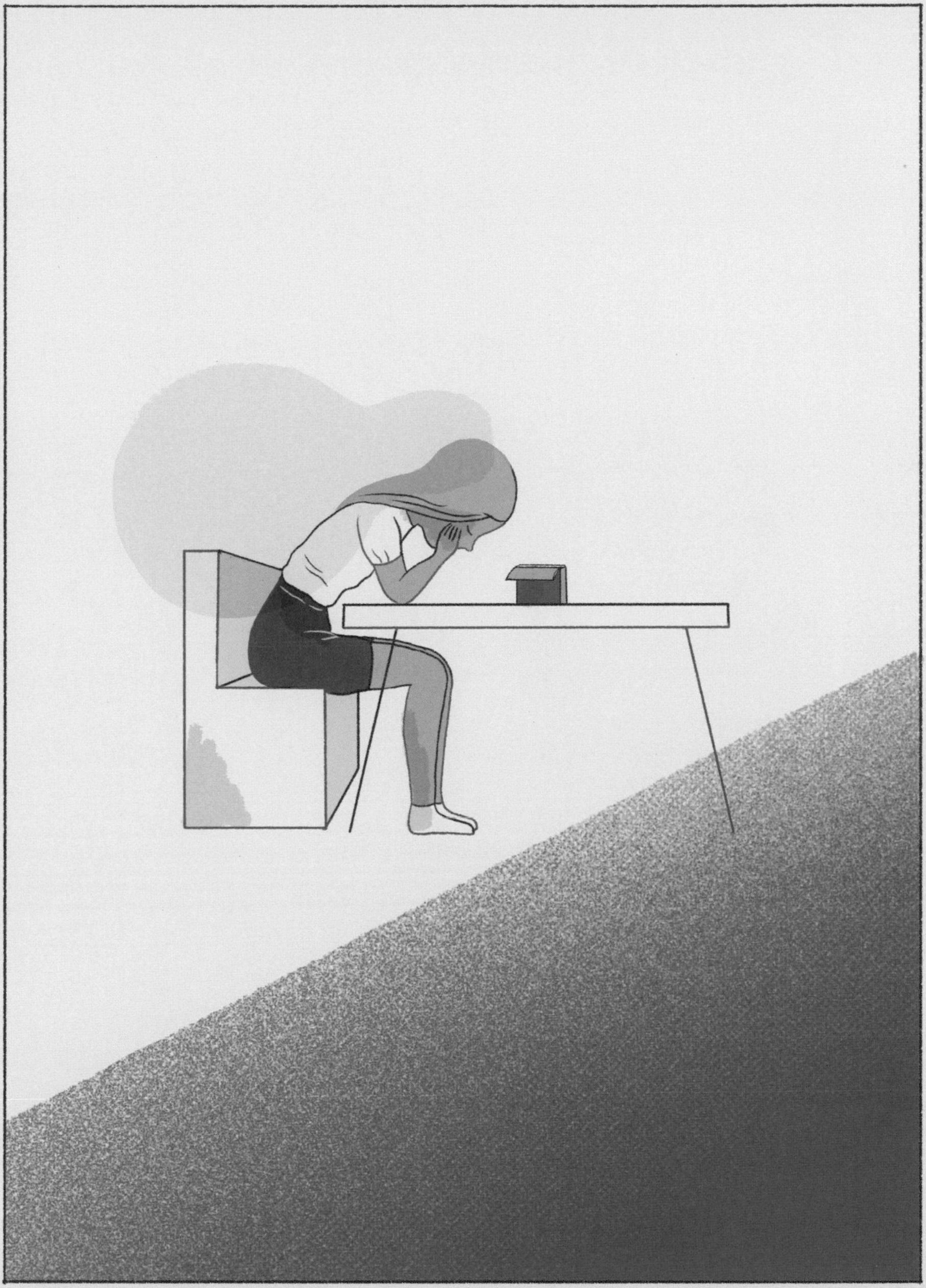

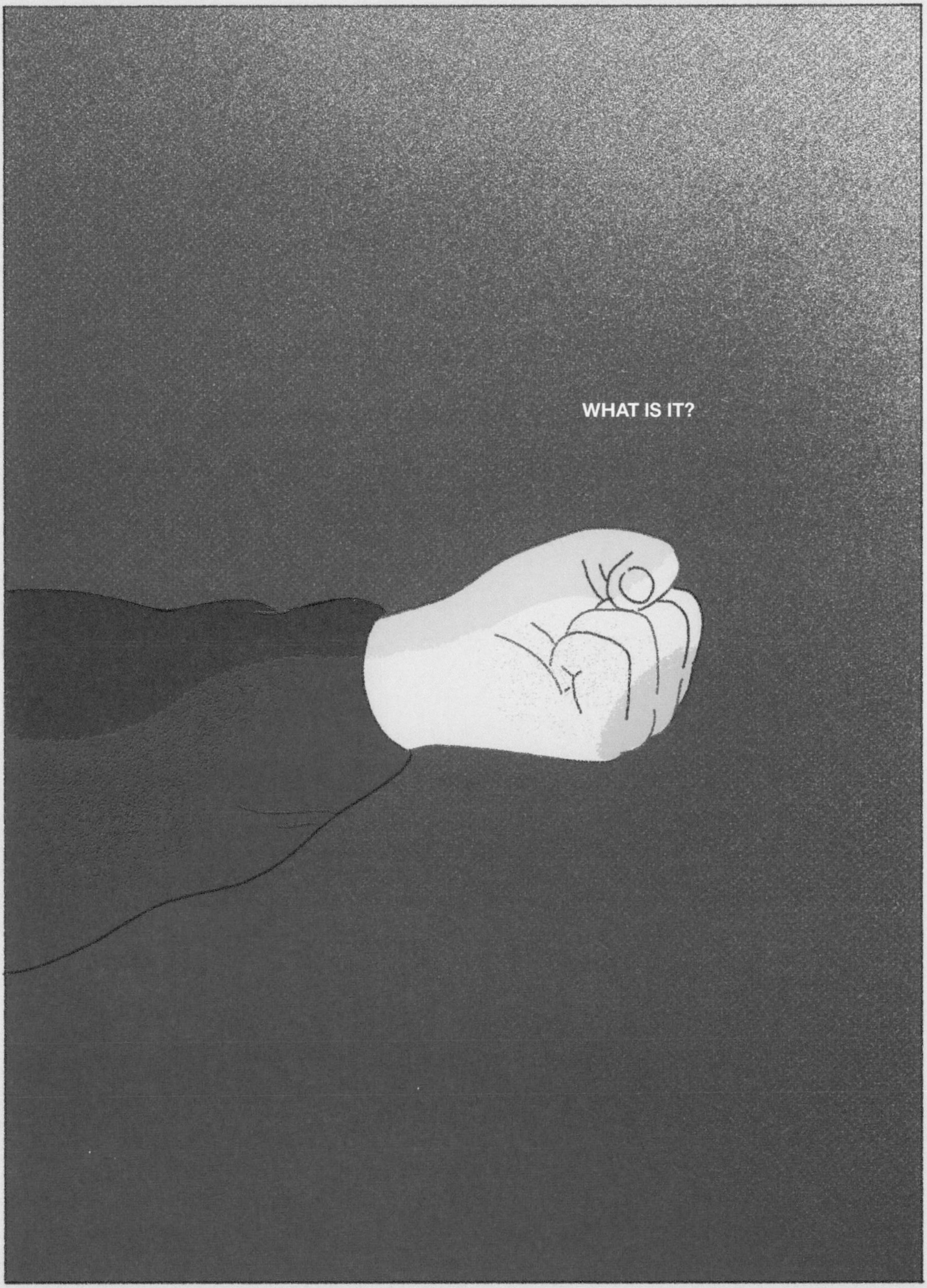
WHAT IS IT?

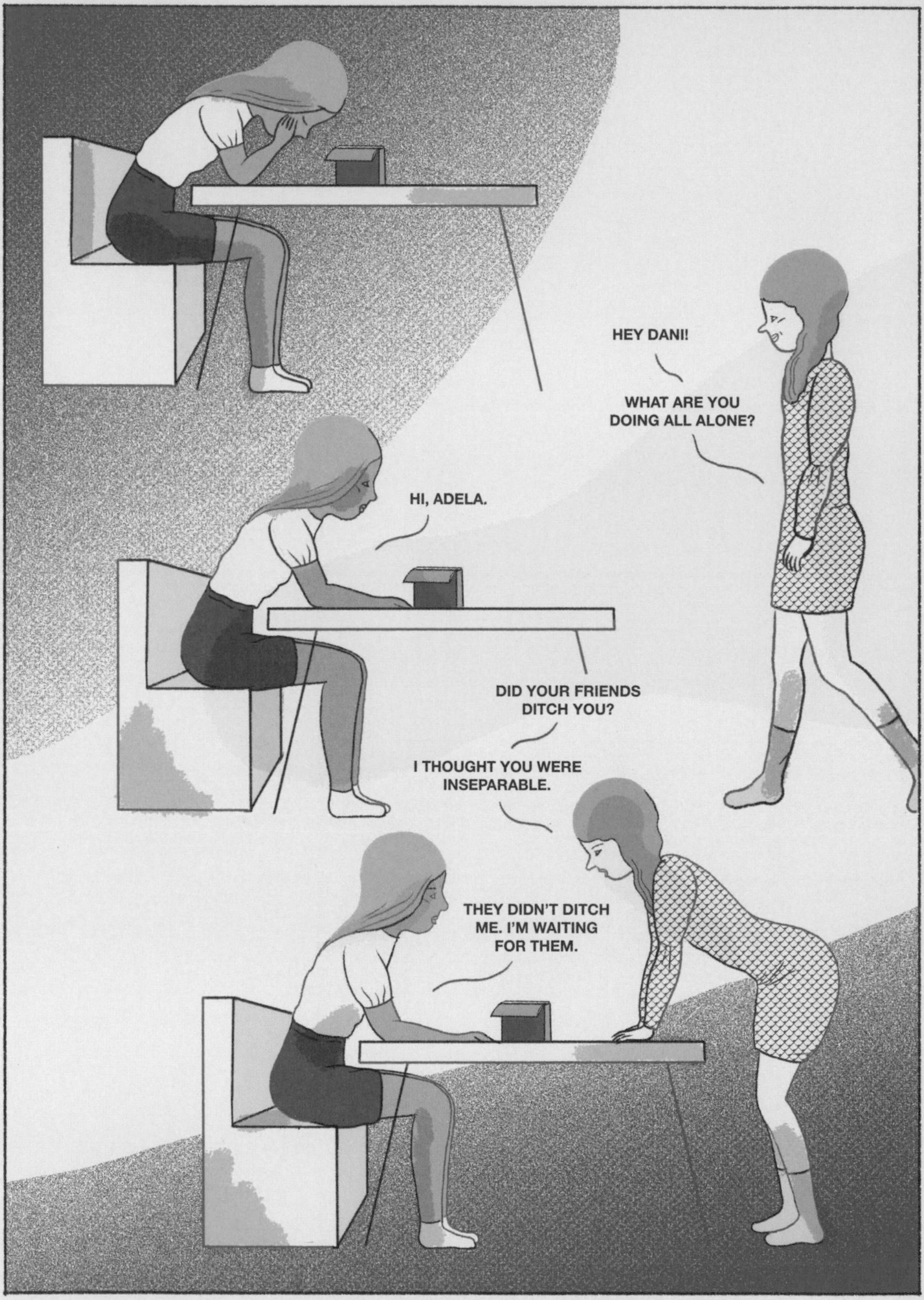
HEY DANI!
WHAT ARE YOU DOING ALL ALONE?
HI, ADELA.
DID YOUR FRIENDS DITCH YOU?
I THOUGHT YOU WERE INSEPARABLE.
THEY DIDN'T DITCH ME. I'M WAITING FOR THEM.

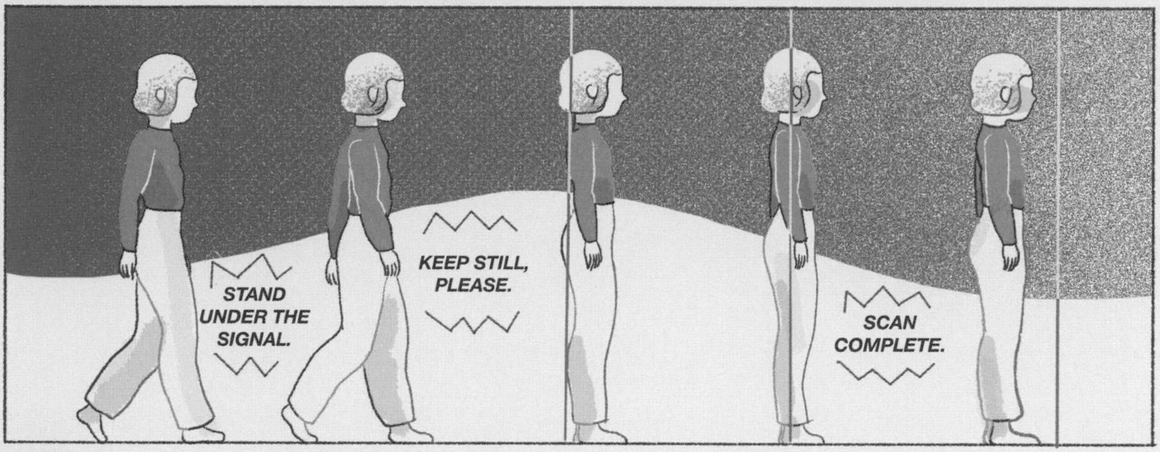
STAND UNDER THE SIGNAL.
KEEP STILL, PLEASE.
SCAN COMPLETE.

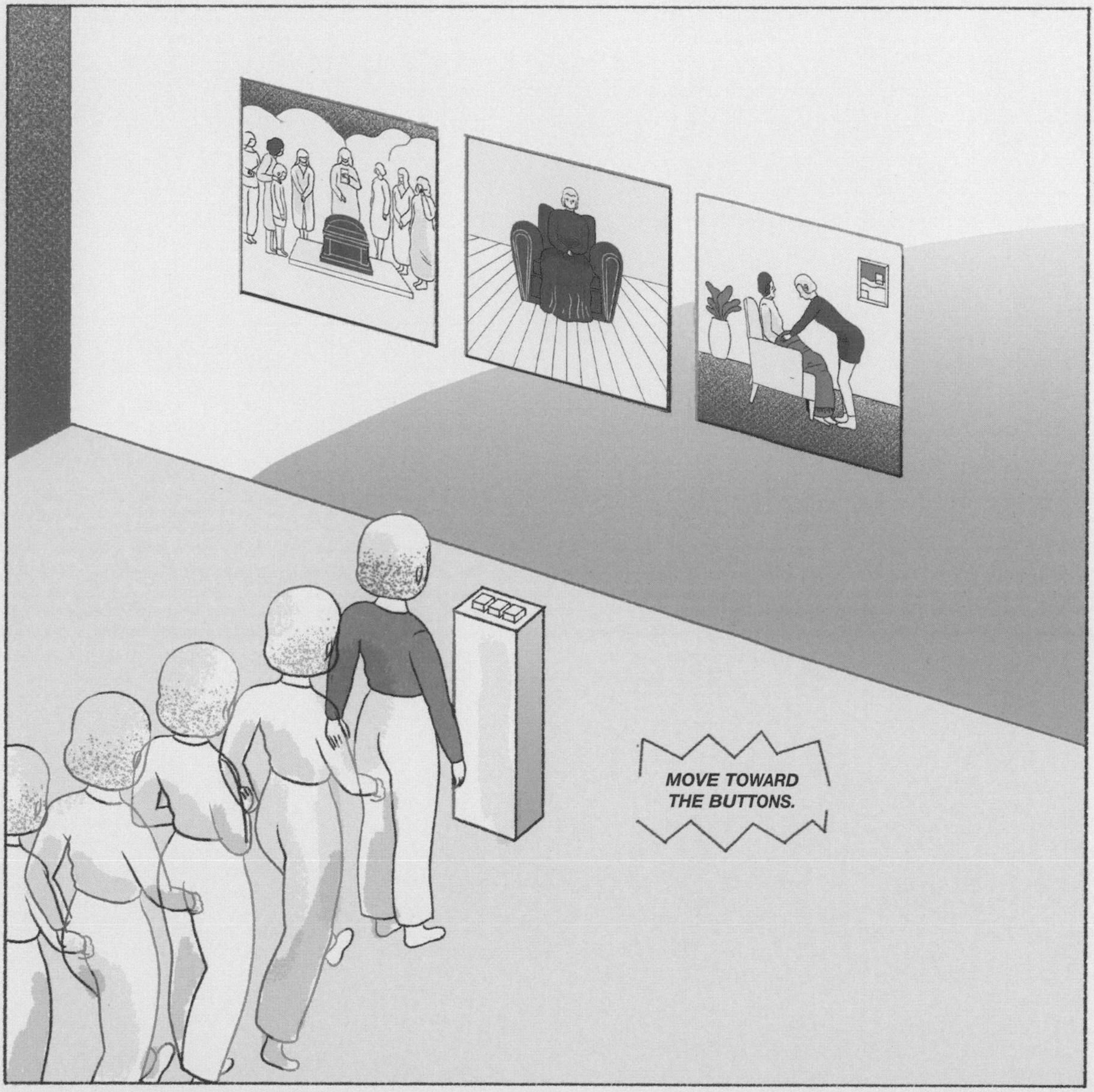
MOVE TOWARD THE BUTTONS.

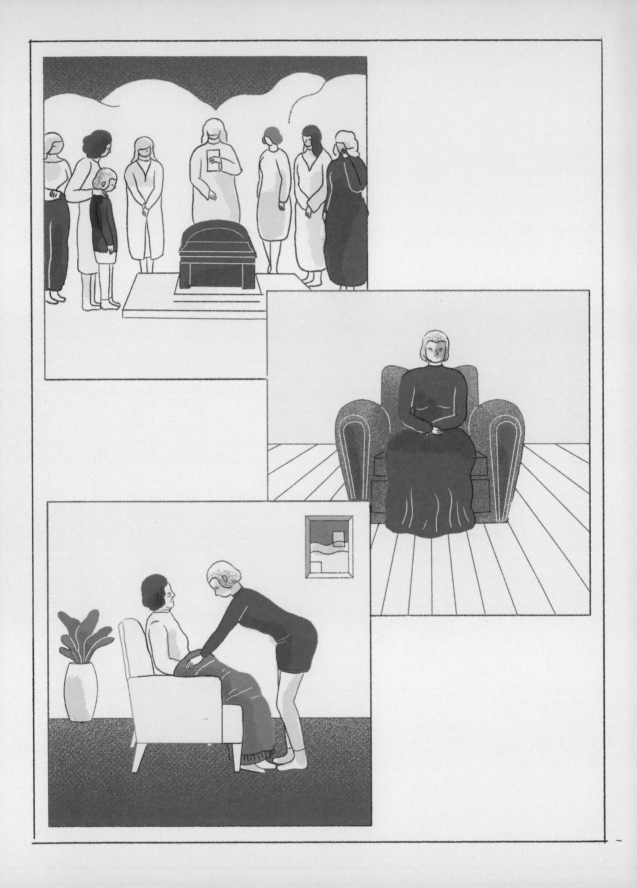

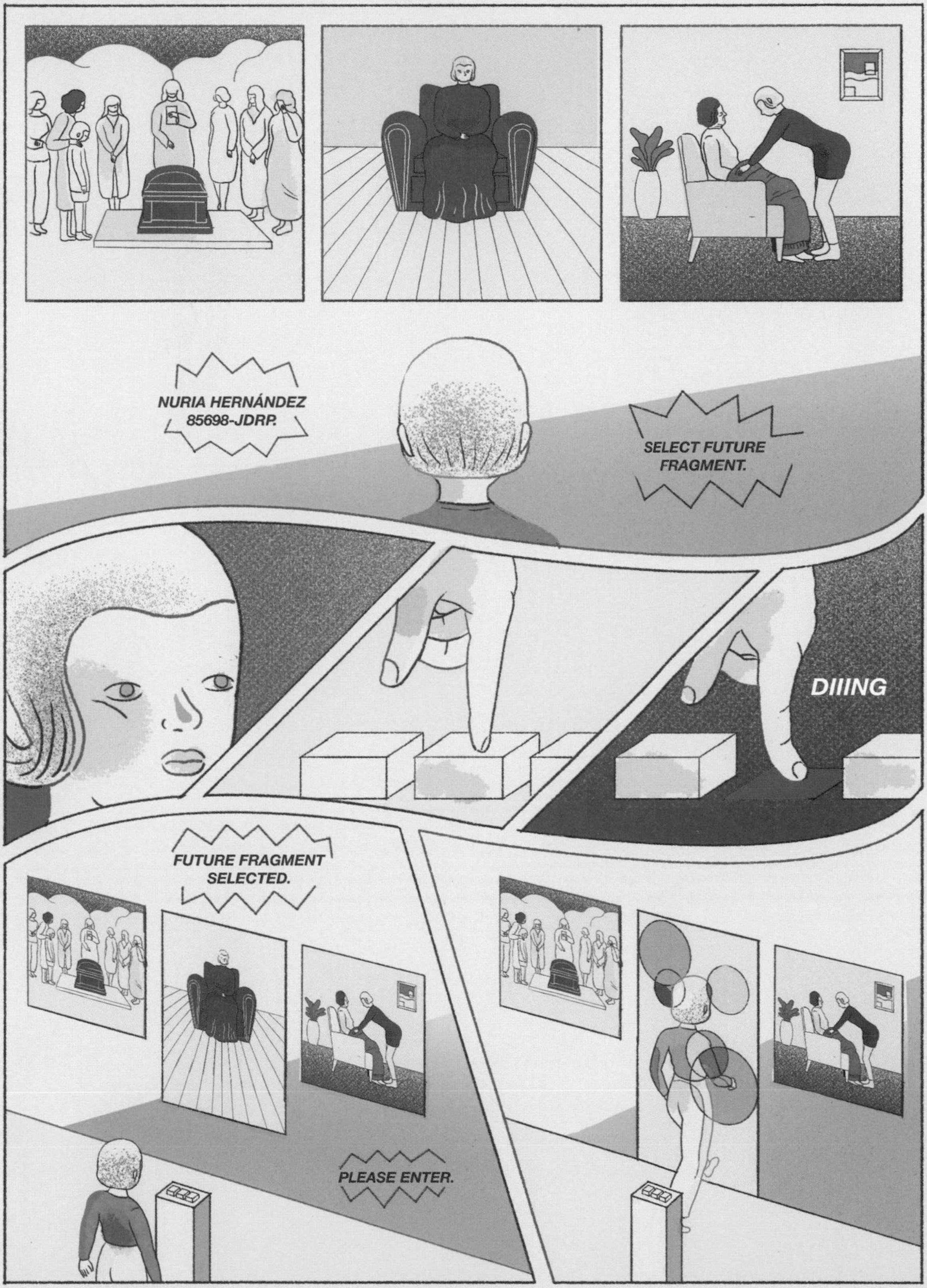
NURIA HERNÁNDEZ
85698-JDRP.
SELECT FUTURE
FRAGMENT.
DIIING
FUTURE FRAGMENT
SELECTED.
PLEASE ENTER.

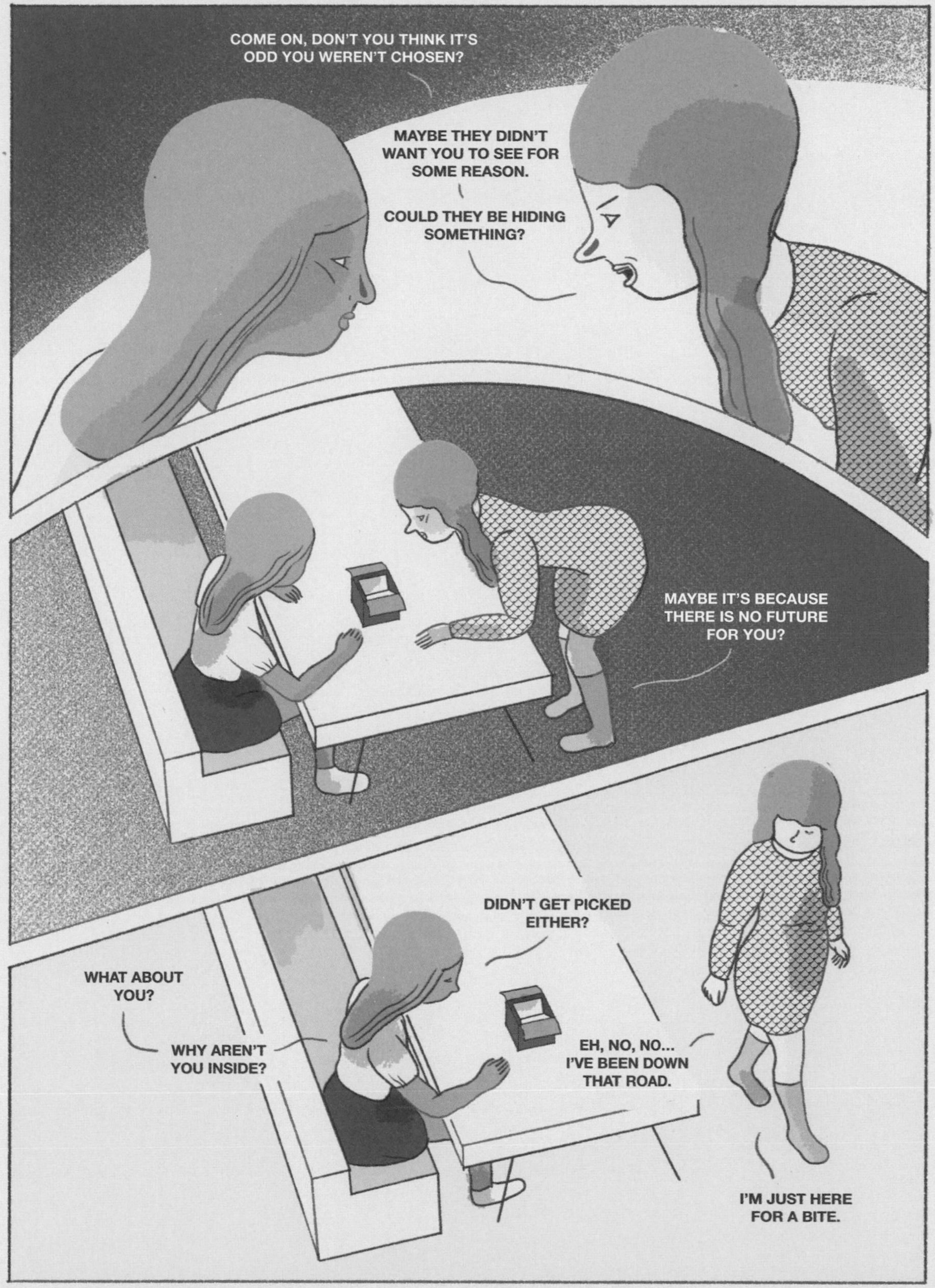
COME ON, DON'T YOU THINK IT'S ODD YOU WEREN'T CHOSEN?
MAYBE THEY DIDN'T WANT YOU TO SEE FOR SOME REASON.
COULD THEY BE HIDING SOMETHING?
MAYBE IT'S BECAUSE THERE IS NO FUTURE FOR YOU?
DIDN'T GET PICKED EITHER?
WHAT ABOUT YOU?
WHY AREN'T YOU INSIDE?
EH, NO, NO... I'VE BEEN DOWN THAT ROAD.
I'M JUST HERE FOR A BITE.

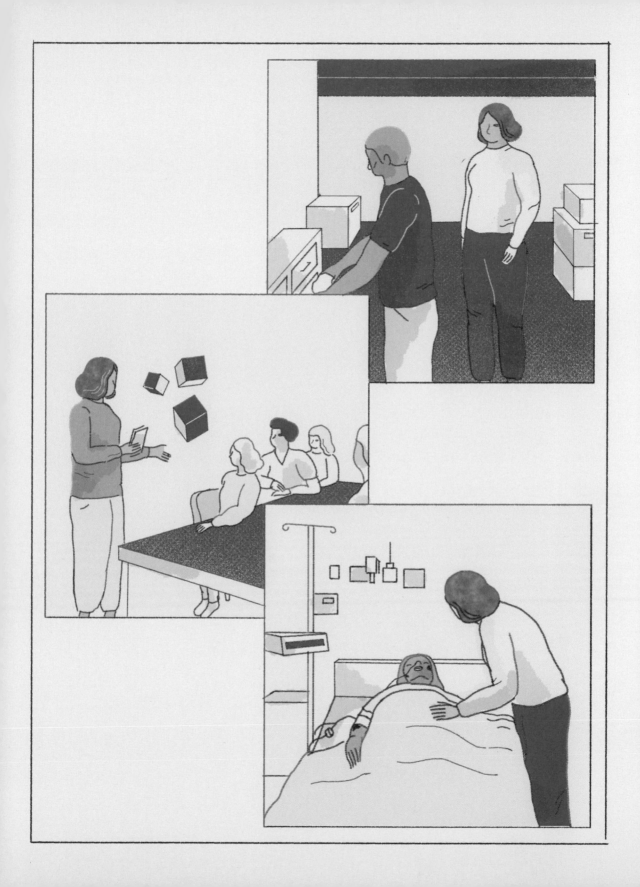

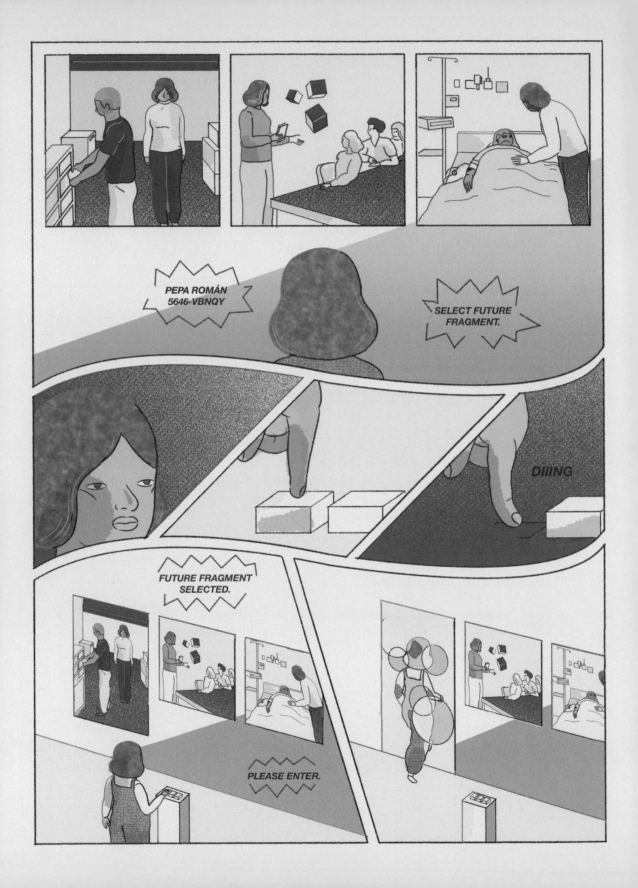

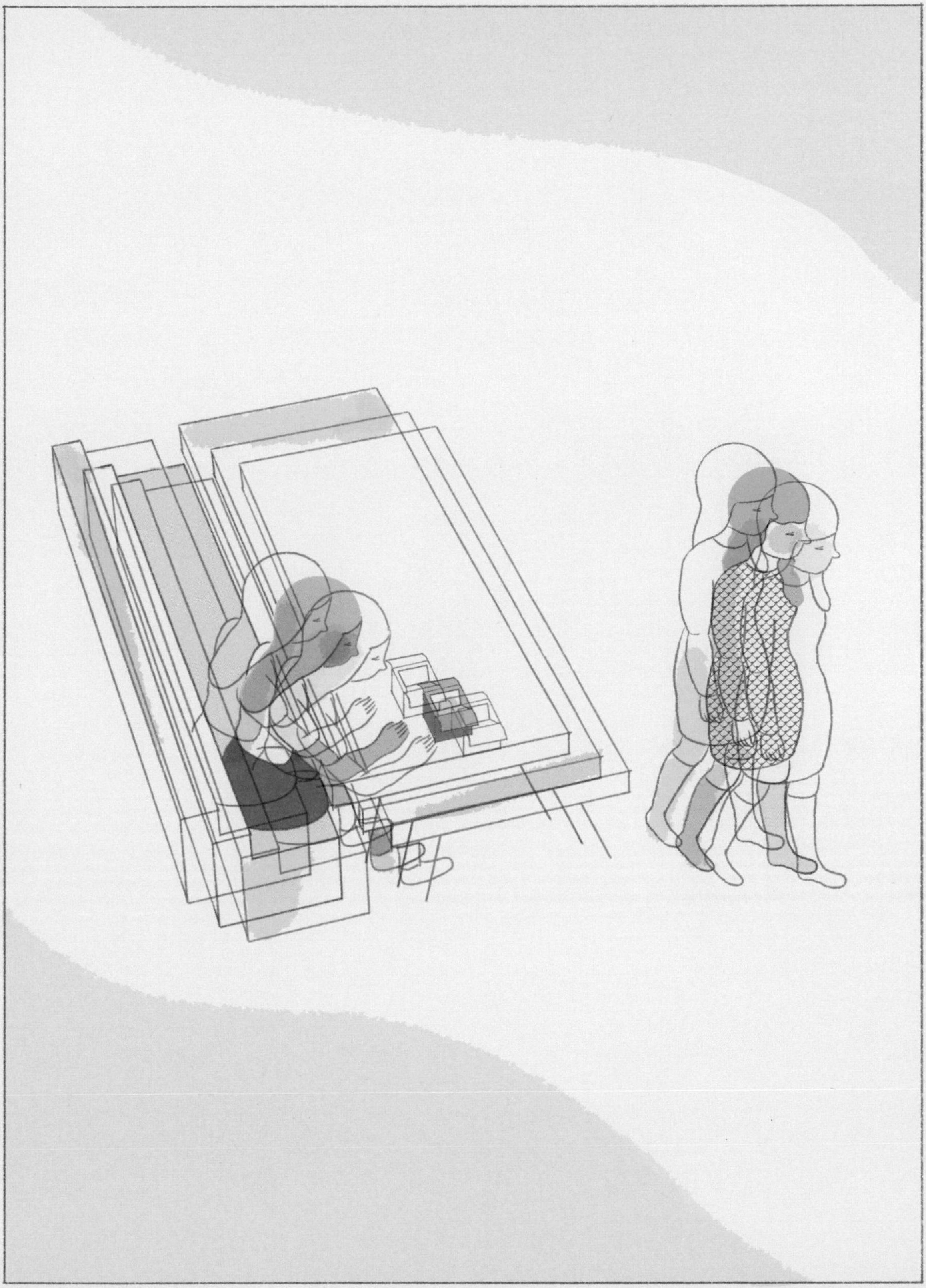

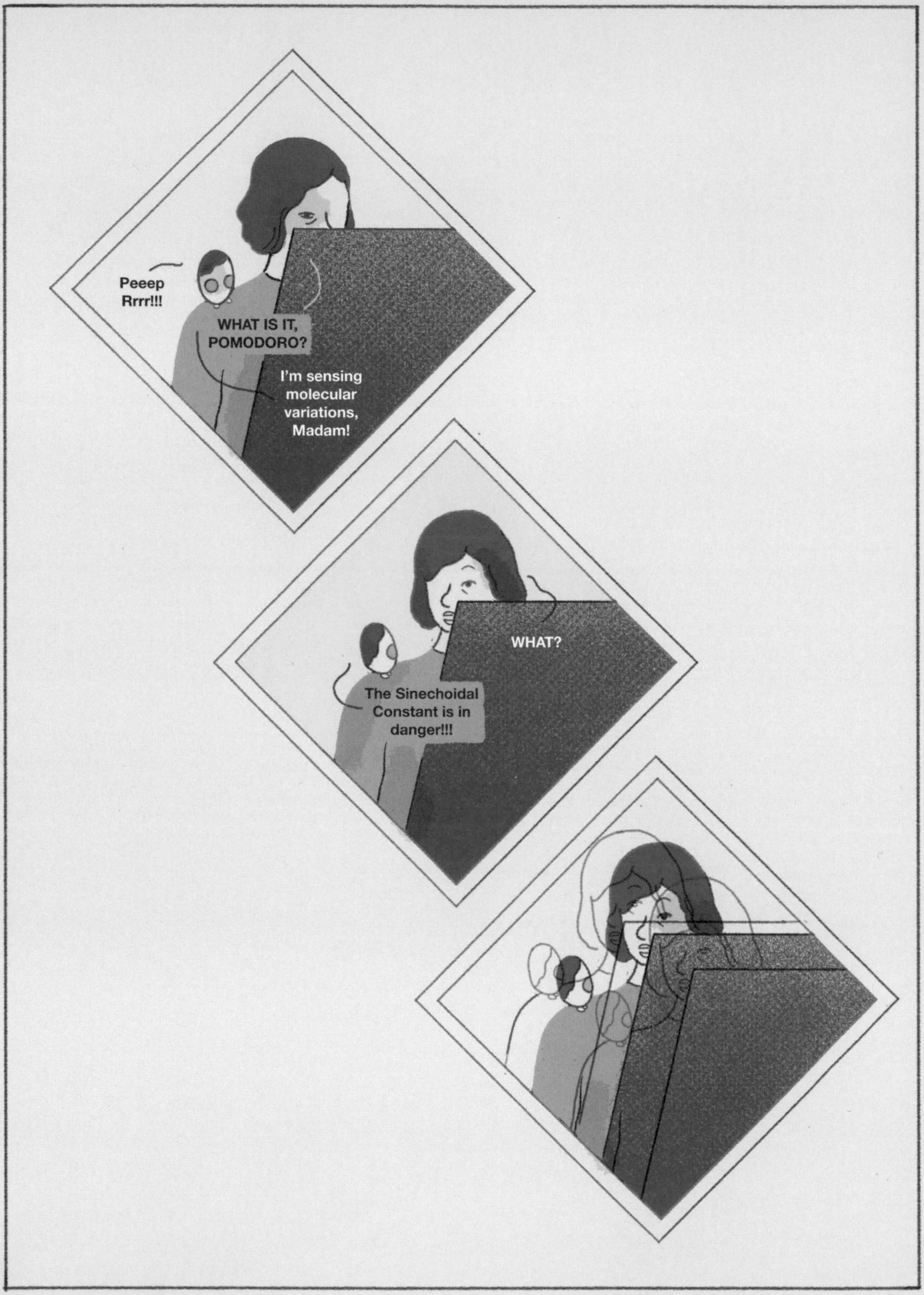
Peeep
Rrrr!!!
WHAT IS IT, POMODORO?
I'm sensing molecular variations, Madam!
WHAT?
The Sinechoidal Constant is in danger!!!

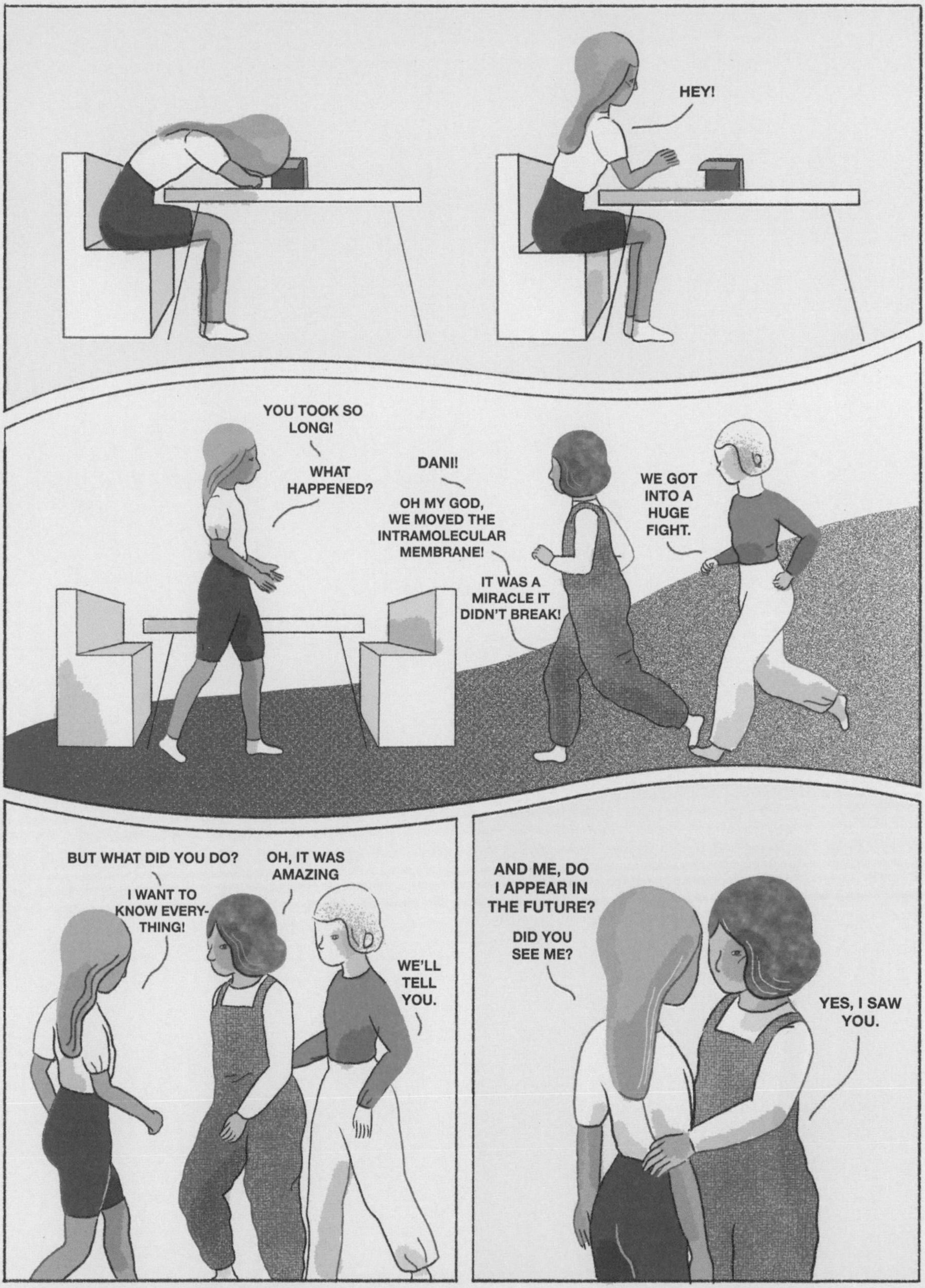
HEY!
YOU TOOK SO LONG!
WHAT HAPPENED?
DANI!
OH MY GOD, WE MOVED THE INTRAMOLECULAR MEMBRANE!
IT WAS A MIRACLE IT DIDN'T BREAK!
WE GOT INTO A HUGE FIGHT.
BUT WHAT DID YOU DO?
I WANT TO KNOW EVERY-THING!
OH, IT WAS AMAZING
WE'LL TELL YOU.
AND ME, DO I APPEAR IN THE FUTURE?
DID YOU SEE ME?
YES, I SAW YOU.

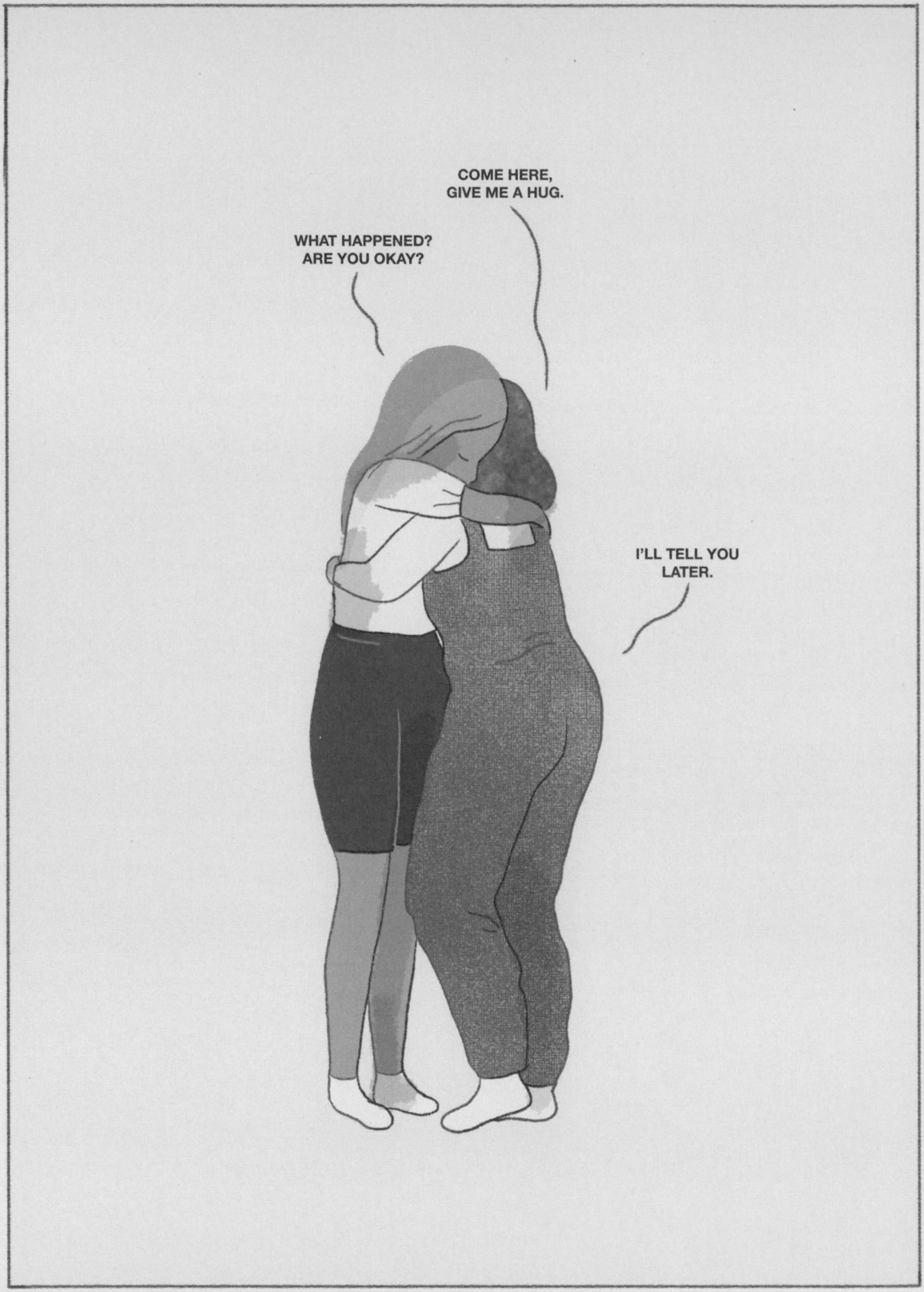
COME HERE,
GIVE ME A HUG.
WHAT HAPPENED?
ARE YOU OKAY?
I'LL TELL YOU
LATER.

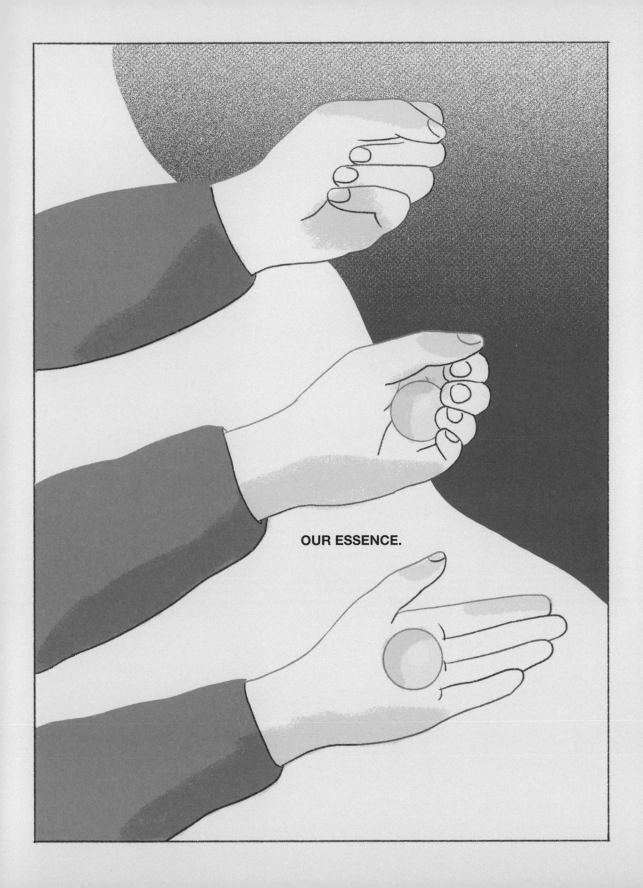

OUR ESSENCE.

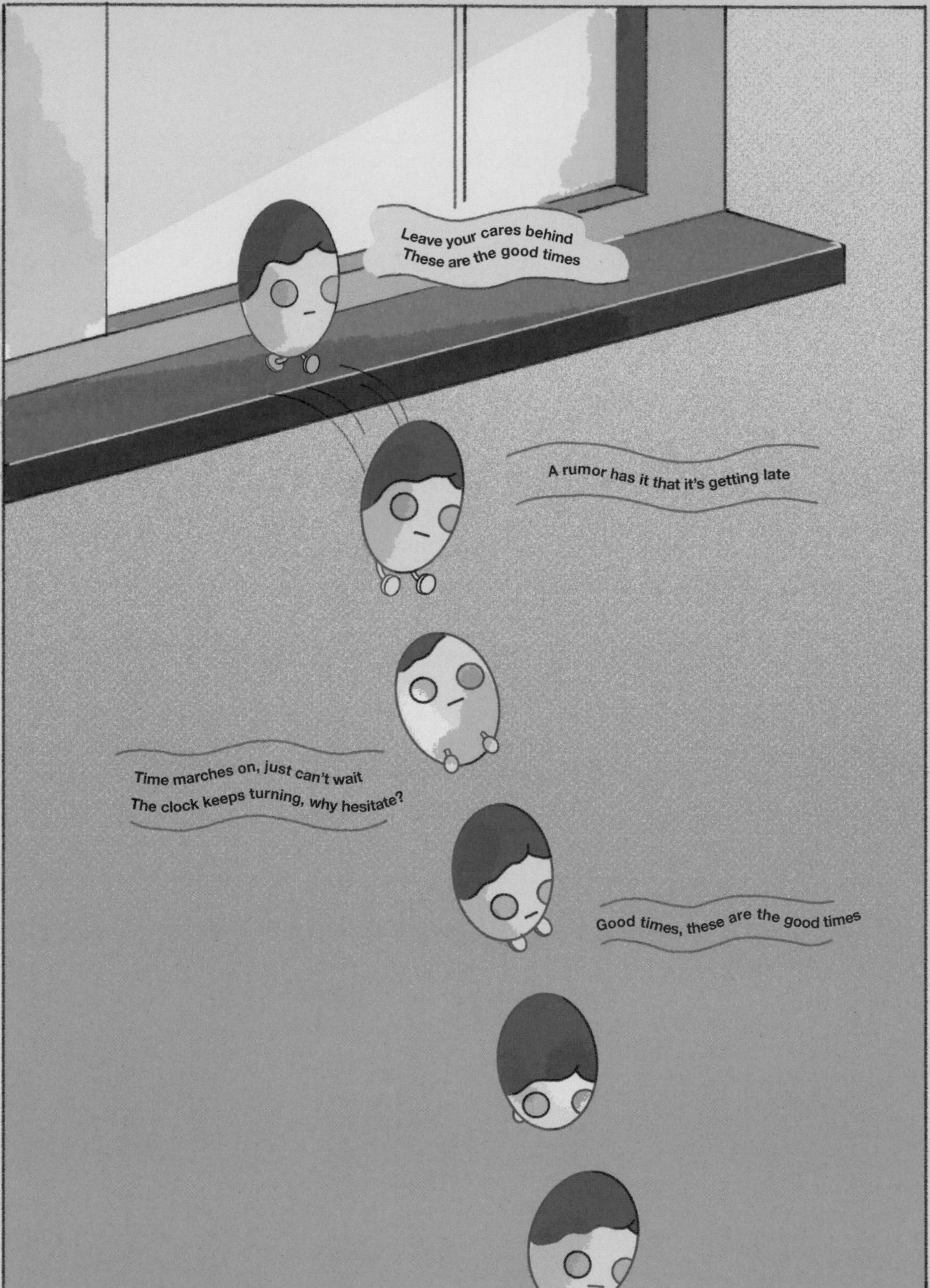
Leave your cares behind
These are the good times
A rumor has it that it's getting late
Time marches on, just can't wait
The clock keeps turning, why hesitate?
Good times, these are the good times

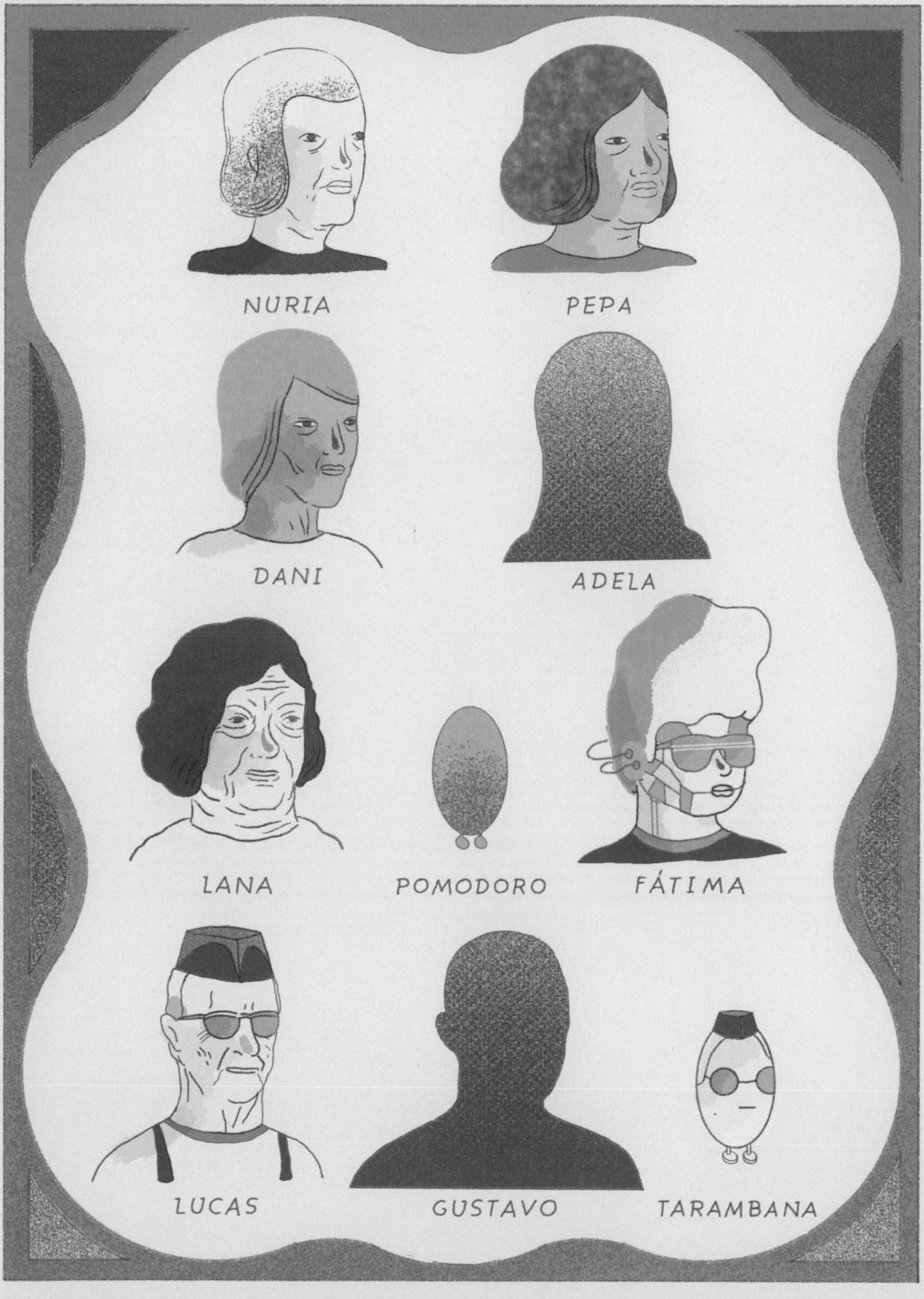
NURIA
PEPA
DANI
ADELA
LANA
POMODORO
FÁTIMA
LUCAS
GUSTAVO
TARAMBANA

**TO ALL THOSE
WHO REALLY
LOVE ME.
THANKS**

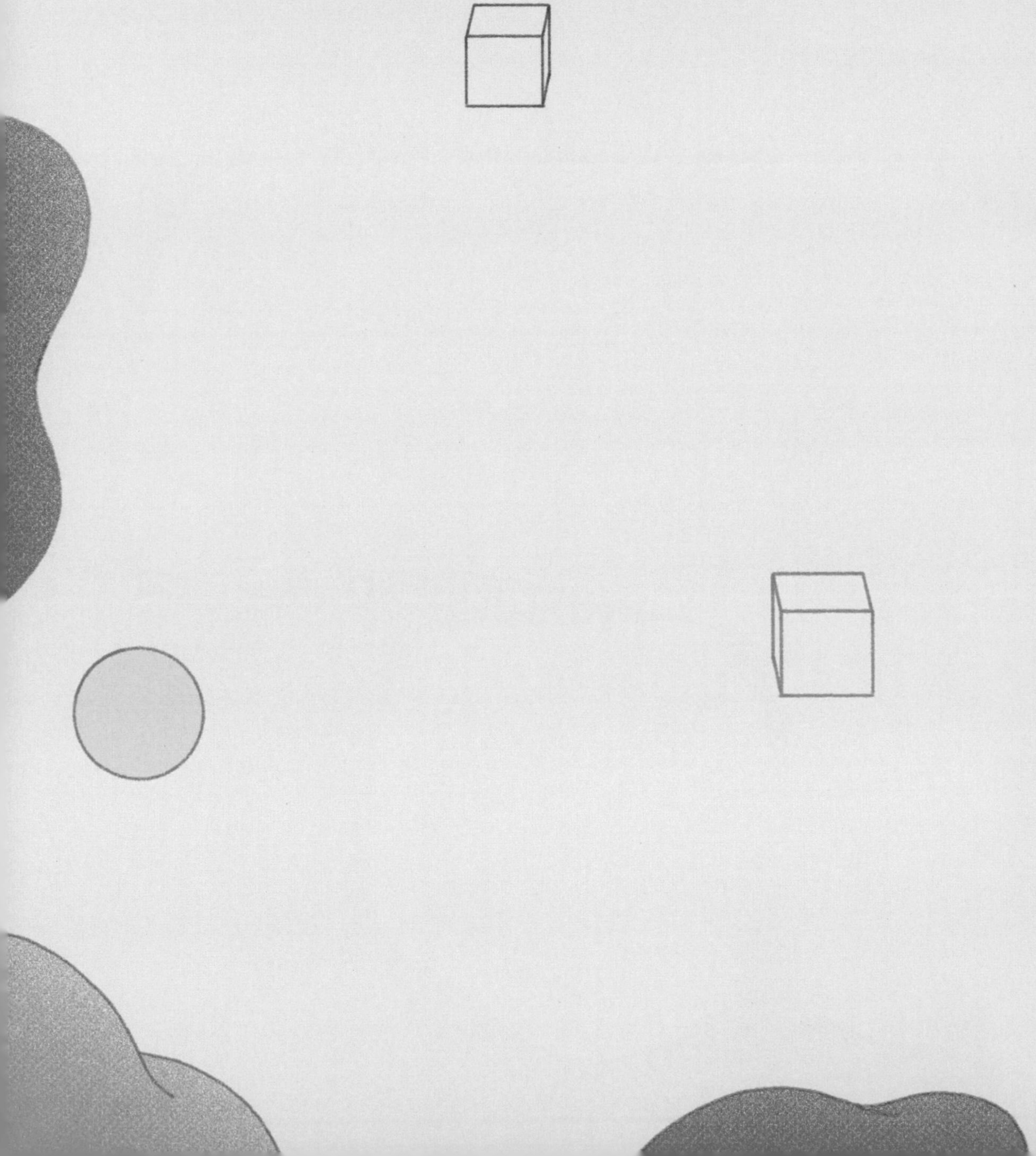

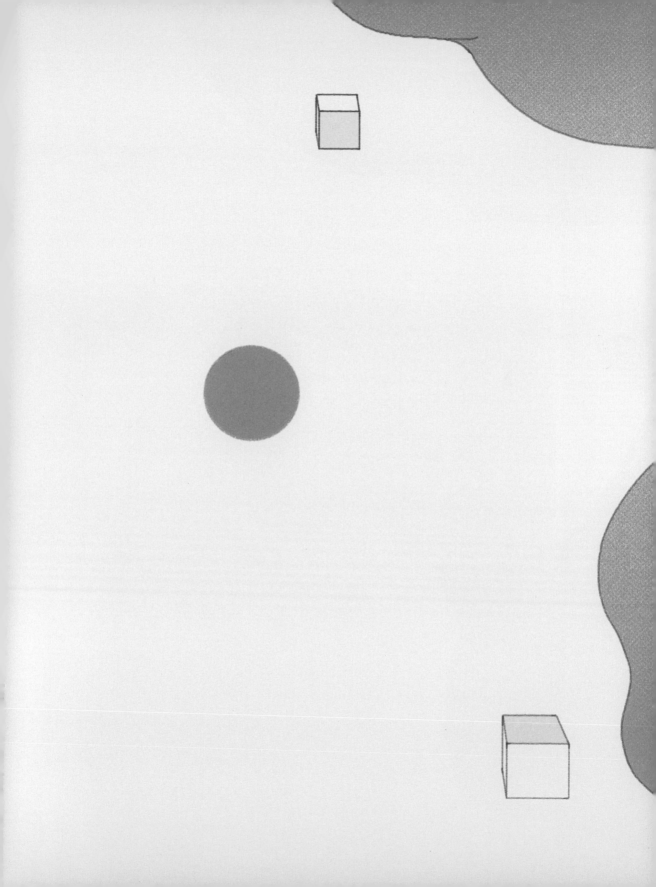

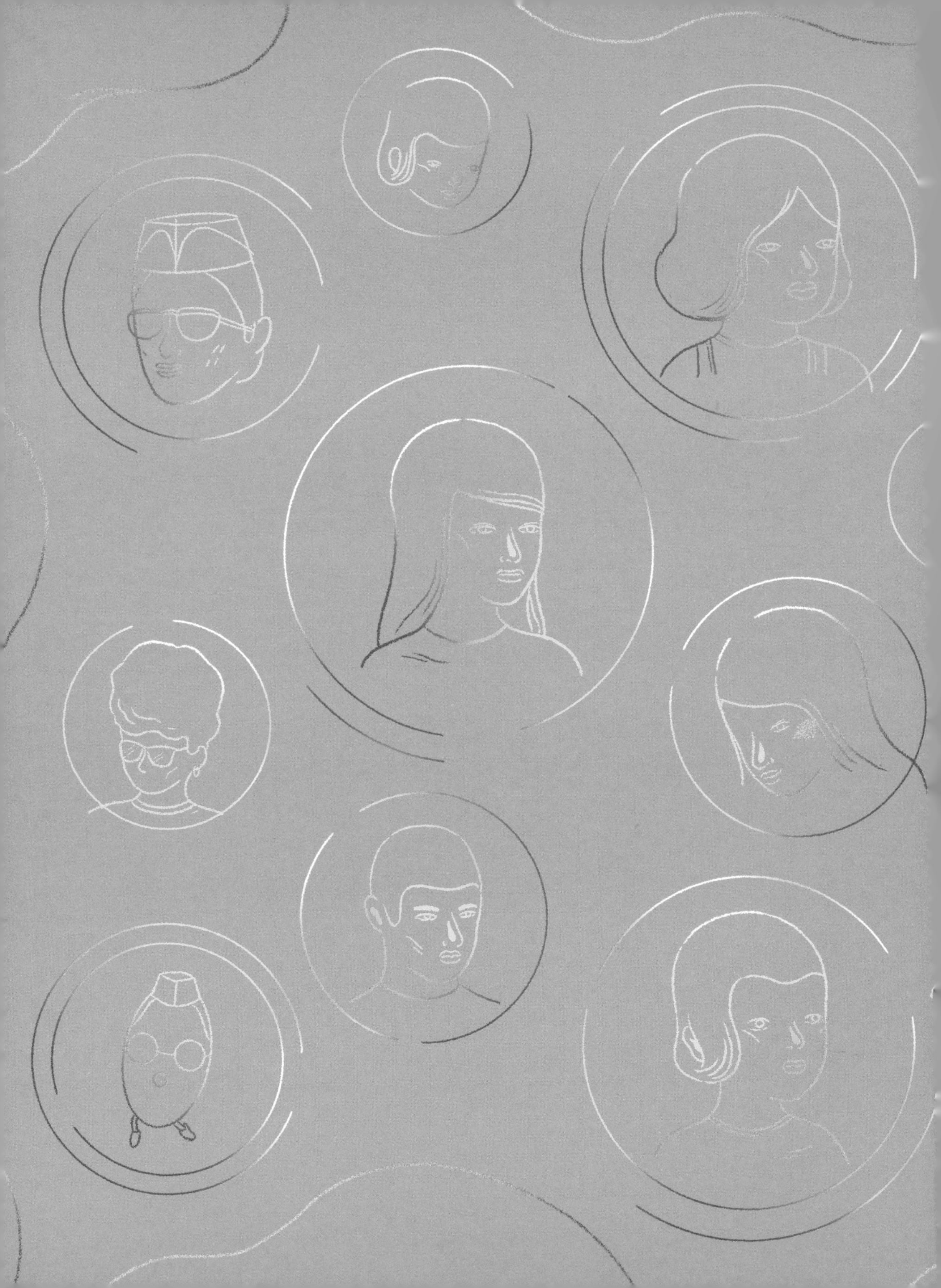